MODERN
CHEMISTRY

CHAPTER TESTS
WITH ANSWER KEY

D1127445

HOLT, RINEHART AND WINSTON

A Harcourt Classroom Education Company

Austin • New York • Orlando • Atlanta • San Francisco • Boston • Dallas • Toronto • London

To the Teacher

This booklet of blackline masters contains a four-page test for each chapter of *Modern Chemistry*. Each test starts with a multiple-choice section. Other sections vary depending on the nature of the material covered in the chapter and may include fill-in-the-blank, matching, short answer, or problems. Test items are designed to evaluate mastery of the section objectives given in the text. Complete answer keys for all 22 Chapter Tests are provided in the back of this book.

Cover: Portion of the periodic table superimposed on a photomicrograph of crystals of the amino-acid dimer cystine. Photo by © Mel Pollinger/Fran Heyl Associates, NYC.

Printed in the United States of America

ISBN 0-03-057357-2

4 5 6 7   862   05 04 03 02

TABLE OF CONTENTS

CHAPTER 1 TEST
Matter and Change

MULTIPLE CHOICE On the line at the left of each statement, write the letter of the choice that best completes the statement or answers the question.

1. _____ Chemistry is a natural science that deals with the study of ____.

    a. living things and their life processes
    b. the physical features of Earth
    c. the composition, structure, properties, and changes of matter
    d. the composition, motion, and relative positions of stars and planets

2. _____ The branch of chemistry that identifies the composition of materials is ____.

    a. biochemistry   **c.** physical chemistry
    b. organic chemistry   **d.** analytical chemistry

3. _____ An example of an extensive property is ____.

    a. mass   **c.** color
    b. density   **d.** boiling point

4. _____ An example of an element is ____.

    a. sugar   **c.** water
    b. soil   **d.** oxygen

5. _____ An example of a heterogeneous mixture is ____.

    a. salt   **c.** mud
    b. nitrogen   **d.** air

6. _____ Which process is a chemical change?

    a. heating to boiling
    b. dissolving in alcohol
    c. burning in air
    d. slicing into two pieces

7. _____ Water boiling at 100°C is an example of a(n) ____.

    a. chemical property   **c.** physical property
    b. extensive property   **d.** chemical change

8. _____ Every pure chemical compound consists of two or more elements ____.

    a. combined chemically
    b. that can be separated by a physical change
    c. that cannot be separated
    d. combined in any proportion

CHAPTER 1 TEST continued

FILL IN THE BLANK Write the correct term (or terms) in the space provided.

9. The two properties that all matter has in common are _____ .

10. In the periodic table, elements in the vertical columns together form a(n)

_____ .

11. A mixture that has the same proportion of components throughout is called

_____ .

12. The substances that are formed by a chemical change are called the

_____ .

13. The element type that is a good conductor of electricity is a(n)

_____ .

14. The state of matter in which a material has a definite volume and a definite shape is the

_____ .

15. Elements are arranged in the periodic table according to their

_____ .

16. The smallest unit of an element that has the properties of that element is a(n)

_____ .

17. When atoms of two or more elements are chemically bonded, the substance formed is a(n)

_____ .

18. If testing shows an element is a poor conductor of electricity, it is a(n)

_____ .

19. A blend of two or more kinds of matter, each of which retains its own identity and properties, is

a(n) _____ .

20. If a material is tested and every sample has exactly the same properties and the same composition,

it is a(n) _____ .

21. _____ research is carried out for the sake of increasing
knowledge.

22. A(n) _____ is an element that has some characteristics of metals
and some characteristics of nonmetals.

CHAPTER 1 TEST continued

For each of the following chemical reactions, identify the reactants and the products.

23. carbon + oxygen → carbon dioxide

reactant(s): _____

product(s): _____

24. mercury(II) oxide → mercury + oxygen

reactant(s): _____

product(s): _____

MATCHING   On the line to the left of each symbol, write the letter of the correct element name.

25. _____ Sr   **a.** silicon

26. _____ Cl   **b.** sodium

27. _____ Co   **c.** cobalt

28. _____ Si   **d.** iron

29. _____ Na   **e.** tin

30. _____ Cu   **f.** strontium

31. _____ Fe   **g.** chlorine

32. _____ Au   **h.** gold

33. _____ Sn   **i.** copper

                          j. silver

Classify each of the following as either a *physical change* or a *chemical change*.

34. _____ melting an ice cube

35. _____ burning a piece of paper

36. _____ slicing a loaf of bread

37. _____ sharpening a pencil

38. _____ decomposing mercury(II) oxide

39. _____ dissolving sugar in water

CHAPTER 1 TEST continued

SHORT ANSWER Write the answers to the following questions in the space provided.

40. Explain the differences between solid, liquid, and gaseous states in terms of the arrangement of the particles.

_____

_____

_____

_____

41. Contrast mixtures and pure substances.

_____

_____

_____

_____

42. State the law of conservation of energy.

_____

_____

_____

_____

43. Contrast heterogeneous and homogeneous mixtures.

_____

_____

_____

_____

44. How could you prove that water is a compound and not an element?

_____

_____

_____

_____

CHAPTER 2 TEST

Measurements and Calculations

MULTIPLE CHOICE On the line at the left of each statement, write the letter of the choice that best completes the statement or answers the question.

1. _____ The four major stages of the scientific method are _____.

   a. observing, formulating hypotheses, testing hypotheses, and theorizing
   b. observing, generalizing, theorizing, and formulating hypotheses
   c. observing, generalizing, theorizing, and testing hypotheses
   d. collecting data, predicting, testing hypotheses, and theorizing

2. _____ By making several measurements with the same balance, a chemist obtained values of 5.224 g, 5.235 g, and 5.259 g for the mass of a sample. Without knowing the actual mass of the sample, we can tell that these measurements have _____.

   a. good precision   **c.** poor precision
   b. good accuracy   **d.** poor accuracy

3. _____ Which equation is an inverse proportion?

   a. $V = \frac{1}{k}T$ **c.** $PV = k$
   b. $F = -kx^2$ **d.** $y = kx - 8$

4. _____ The distance between the sun and Earth is 150 million km. Light travels at a speed of 3.0×10^8 m/s. Dividing the distance by the speed and multiplying by the number of meters in a kilometer will result in units of _____.

   a. seconds   **c.** kilometers squared
   b. meters per second   **d.** kilometers per second

5. _____ The measurement that has only nonsignificant zeros is _____.

   a. 506 mL   **c.** 0.0037 mL
   b. 60.0 mL   **d.** 400. mL

6. _____ If some measurements agree closely but differ widely from the actual value, these measurements are _____.

   a. both accurate and precise   **c.** precise but not accurate
   b. neither precise nor accurate   **d.** accurate but not precise

7. _____ If two quantities are directly proportional, when one quantity increases by 10 percent, the other _____.

   a. increases by 10 percent   **c.** stays the same
   b. decreases by 10 percent   **d.** may increase at a different rate

8. _____ In division and multiplication, the answer must not have more significant figures than the _____.

   a. number in the calculation with the fewest significant figures
   b. number in the calculation with the most significant figures
   c. average number of significant figures in the problem
   d. total number of significant figures in the problem

In each of the following measurements, name the quantity being measured.

example: _____*temperature*_____ 300 K

9. _____ 22 s

10. _____ 3.5 mg

11. _____ 1.59 g/mL

12. _____ 16 J

13. _____ 34.5 km

14. _____ 0.75 mL

15. _____ 3.66 m^2

Identify the following data as *qualitative* or *quantitative*.

16. _____ The solid dissolves in water.

17. _____ The temperature of the solution is 3°C.

18. _____ The solution is dark blue.

19. _____ The density of the solution is 1.13 g/mL.

FILL IN THE BLANK   Write the correct term or value in the space provided.

20. The speed of light is 300 000 km/s. This number equals _____ km/s when it is written in scientific notation.

21. The quantity 0.202 g has _____ significant figures.

22. If two figures are significant, how should the measurement 0.0255 g be reported?

_____.

23. A Florence flask can contain 250. mL of liquid. Expressed in scientific notation, the capacity of the

flask in liters is _____.

24. A(n) _____ is something that has magnitude, size, or amount.

25. SI base units can be combined to form _____.

26. To change from one unit to another, you must first determine the appropriate

_____.

CHAPTER 2 TEST continued

Convert the following measurements. Write your answer on the line to the left.

27. _____ kg = 43.2 g

28. _____ mL = 5.4 L

29. _____ K = 27°C

30. _____ J = 250. cal (1 cal = 4.184 J)

31. _____ cm = 3.51×10^{10} nm

SHORT ANSWER   Write the answers to the following questions in the space provided.

32. How does a theory differ from a hypothesis?

_____

_____

_____

33. How does weight differ from mass?

_____

_____

_____

34. How are models used in science?

_____

_____

_____

35. Describe the graph of two quantities that are directly proportional and the graph of two quantities that are inversely proportional.

_____

_____

_____

_____

_____

PROBLEMS Write the answers to the questions on the line to the left, and show your work in the space provided. Express each answer to the correct number of significant digits.

36. _____ The mass of a 5.00 cm³ sample of clay is 11.0 g. What is the density of the clay?

37. _____ A length measurement is 1.40 cm. The correct value is 1.36 cm. Calculate the percent error.

38. _____ The density of lead is 11.35 g/cm³. What is the mass of a 10.0 cm³ piece of lead?

39. _____ What is the volume in liters of a cube whose edge is 4.33 cm long?

40. _____ What is the sum of 3.089 g and 0.07452 g?

Name _____ Date _____ Class _____

CHAPTER 3 TEST
Atoms: The Building Blocks of Matter

MULTIPLE CHOICE On the line at the left of each statement, write the letter of the choice that best completes the statement or answers the question.

1. _____ The behavior of cathode rays in a glass tube containing gas at low pressure led scientists to conclude that the rays were composed of _____.

    a. energy   **c.** negative particles

    b. positive particles   **d.** neutral particles

2. _____ The basic principles of atomic theory that are still recognized today were first conceived by _____.

    a. Avogadro   **c.** Dalton

    b. Bohr   **d.** Rutherford

3. _____ An example of the law of multiple proportions is the existence of _____.

    a. $FeCl_3$ and $Fe(SO_4)_3$ **c.** CO and CO_2

    b. O_2 and O_3 **d.** $FeCl_2$ and $Fe(NO_3)_2$

4. _____ Atoms of the same element can differ in _____.

    a. chemical properties

    b. mass number

    c. atomic number

    d. number of protons and electrons

5. _____ Dalton's atomic theory helped to explain the law of conservation of mass because it stated that atoms _____.

    a. could not combine   **c.** all had the same mass

    b. were invisible   **d.** could not be created or destroyed

6. _____ Milliken's experiments determined _____.

    a. that the electron carried no charge

    b. that the electron carried the smallest possible positive charge

    c. the approximate value of the electron's mass

    d. that the electron had no mass

7. _____ In Rutherford's experiment, a small percentage of the positively charged particles bombarding the metal's surface _____.

    a. were slightly deflected as they passed through the metal

    b. were deflected back toward the source from the metal

    c. passed straight through the metal

    d. combined with the metal

8. _____ Most of the volume of an atom is made up of the _____.

    a. nucleus   **c.** electron cloud

    b. nuclides   **d.** protons

FILL IN THE BLANK   Write the correct term (or terms) in the space provided.

9. If a particular compound is composed of elements A and B, the ratio of the mass of B to the mass of A will always be the same. This is a statement of the law of

   _____.

10. The amount of a substance that contains a number of particles equal to the number of atoms in

    exactly 12 g of carbon-12 is referred to as a(n) _____.

11. Since any metal cathode used in a cathode-ray tube produced the same charged particles, it was

    concluded that all atoms contain _____.

12. The smallest particle of an element that retains the chemical properties of that element is a(n)

    _____.

13. Atoms of one element that have different masses are called

    _____.

14. The total number of protons and neutrons in the nucleus of an isotope is called its

    _____ number.

15. The short-range attractive forces that hold the nuclear particles together are called

    _____.

16. The number of protons in the nucleus of an element is called its

    _____ number.

17. If two or more compounds are composed of elements A and B, the ratio of the masses of B combined with 1 g of A make each compound a ratio of small whole numbers. This is a statement

    of the law of _____.

18. Dalton's atomic theory agreed with the modern atomic theory EXCEPT for the statement that

    all atoms of the same element have the same _____.

Complete the following table to compare the types of subatomic particles.

	Particle	Mass number	Relative charge	Location
19.	Proton			
20.	Neutron			
21.	Electron			

CHAPTER 3 TEST continued

SHORT ANSWER Write the answers to the following questions in the space provided.

22. Give three of the main concepts in Dalton's atomic theory.

_____

_____

_____

_____

23. What is molar mass? How is it related to atomic mass?

_____

_____

_____

_____

24. Explain why the atomic mass of a particular isotope of an element differs from the average atomic mass of that element.

_____

_____

_____

_____

PROBLEMS Write the answers to the questions on the line to the left, and show your work in the space provided.

25. _____ The atomic number of nickel-60 is 28. How many neutrons does this isotope have?

26. _____ Carbon-14 has 8 neutrons. What is the atomic number of carbon-14?

27. _____ An atom of silicon-30 contains 14 protons. How many electrons does it have?

28. _____ Oxygen has three naturally occurring isotopes in the following proportions: oxygen-16, 99.762% (15.994 91 amu); oxygen-17, 0.038000% (16.999 13 amu); oxygen-18, 0.20000% (17.999 16 amu). What is the average atomic mass of oxygen?

29. _____ The average atomic mass of chromium is 52.00 amu. What is the mass of 3.00 mol of chromium?

30. _____ How many moles are in a sample of 63.658 g of carbon? (The molar mass of carbon is 12.01 g/mol.)

31. _____ The mass of a sample of nickel (average atomic mass 58.69 amu) is 11.74 g. How many atoms does it contain?

32. _____ The atomic mass of sulfur is 32.06 amu. How many atoms are present in exactly 2 mol sulfur?

CHAPTER 4 TEST

Arrangement of Electrons in Atoms

MULTIPLE CHOICE On the line at the left of each statement, write the letter of the choice that best completes the statement or answers the question.

1. _____ The principal quantum number of an electron is 4. What are the possible angular momentum quantum numbers?

    a. $\frac{1}{2}, -\frac{1}{2}$ **c.** 0, 1, 2, 3

    b. $-3, -2, -1, 0, 1, 2, 3$ **d.** 4

2. _____ What is the total number of electrons needed to fill the fourth main energy level?

    a. 4   **c.** 16

    b. 8   **d.** 32

3. _____ An orbital that would never exist in the quantum description of an atom is _____.

    a. $3d$ **c.** $6d$

    b. $8s$ **d.** $3f$

4. _____ Whenever an excited hydrogen atom falls back from an excited state to its ground state, it _____.

    a. absorbs a photon of radiation

    b. emits a photon of radiation

    c. emits radiation over a range of frequencies

    d. absorbs specific frequencies of light

5. _____ The wave theory of light best explains the _____.

    a. photoelectric effect

    b. emission of electromagnetic radiation by a hot body

    c. interference of light

    d. Lyman, Balmer, and Paschen series

6. _____ When electrons change energy states, the amount of energy given off or absorbed is equal to _____.

    a. hc **c.** n

    b. hv **d.** cv

7. _____ Max Planck proposed that a "hot" object radiated energy in small, specific amounts called _____.

    a. quanta   **c.** hertz

    b. waves   **d.** electrons

8. _____ Which of the following requires that each of the *p* orbitals at a particular level have one electron before any of them can have two electrons?

    a. Hund's rule   **c.** the Aufbau principle

    b. the Pauli exclusion principle   **d.** the quantum rule

CHAPTER 4 TEST continued

FILL IN THE BLANK   Write the correct term (or terms) in the space provided.

9. A particle that has an outer main energy level fully occupied by eight electrons has a

_____ configuration.

10. The energy of a photon depends on the _____ of
the radiation.

11. If electromagnetic radiation A has a lower frequency than electromagnetic radiation B, then com-

pared with B, the wavelength of A is _____.

12. In SI, the frequency of electromagnetic radiation is measured in

_____.

13. The distance between corresponding points on a wave is called

_____.

14. The ejection of electrons by metals when light shines on them is called the

_____.

15. The lowest energy state of an atom is called its

_____.

16. The number of waves that pass a point per second is called the

_____.

17. When an electron drops from a higher-energy state to a lower-energy state, a(n)

_____ spectrum is produced.

18. The numerical value of the speed of electromagnetic radiation in a vacuum is

_____.

19. _____ is the color of the visible spectrum with the
lowest frequency.

20. The _____ states that it is not possible to know the
velocity and the position of a small particle at the same time.

21. Electrons that are NOT in the highest occupied energy level are called

_____.

22. Any form of energy that exhibits wavelike behavior as it travels through space is called

_____.

Name _____ Date _____ Class _____

CHAPTER 4 TEST continued

MATCHING On the line at the left of each expression in the first column, write the letter of the expression in the second column that is most closely related.

23. _____ An electron occupies the lowest energy orbital that can receive it.

    a. Hund's rule

24. _____ Orbitals of equal energy are occupied by one electron before any orbital is occupied by a second electron.

    b. Pauli exclusion principle

25. _____ No two electrons in the same atom can have the same four quantum numbers.

    c. Bohr model of the atom

26. _____ The single electron of hydrogen orbits the nucleus only in allowed orbits, each with a fixed energy.

    d. Aufbau principle

SHORT ANSWER Write the answers to the following questions in the space provided.

27. What two early twentieth-century observations involving the interaction of light and matter could not be explained by classical theory?

_____

_____

28. Use the Bohr model of the hydrogen atom to explain the emission spectrum of hydrogen.

_____

_____

_____

_____

_____

Write the electron-configuration notation for the following elements in the space provided.

29. fluorine, atomic number 9 _____

30. sulfur, atomic number 16 _____

31. calcium, atomic number 20 _____

32. iron, atomic number 26 _____

Write the noble-gas notation for the following elements in the space provided.

33. carbon, atomic number 6 _____

34. neon, atomic number 10 _____

35. barium, atomic number 56 _____

36. potassium, atomic number 19 _____

Write the orbital notation for the following elements in the space provided.

37. lithium, atomic number 3 _____

38. carbon, atomic number 6 _____

39. neon, atomic number 10 _____

PROBLEMS Write the answers to the questions on the line to the left, and show your work in the space provided.

40. _____ The wavelength of light in the infrared region is 4.257×10^{-7} cm. What is the frequency of this light?

41. _____ The distance from Earth to the moon is approximately 3.84×10^5 km. How long would it take a radio wave with frequency 7.25×10^5 Hz to travel from Earth to the moon?

42. _____ The hydrogen-line emission spectrum includes a line at a wavelength of 434 nm. What is the energy of this radiation? ($h = 6.626 \times 10^{-34}$ J · s)

CHAPTER 5 TEST

The Periodic Law

MULTIPLE CHOICE On the line at the left of each statement, write the letter of the choice that best completes the statement or answers the question.

1. _____ In his periodic table, Mendeleev did not always list elements in order of increasing atomic mass because he wanted to group elements with similar ____ together.

    a. properties   **c.** densities
    b. atomic numbers   **d.** colors

2. _____ The discovery of the noble gases changed Mendeleev's periodic table by adding a new ____.

    a. period   **c.** group
    b. series   **d.** sublevel block

3. _____ Moseley discovered that elements with similar properties occurred at regular intervals when the elements were arranged in order of increasing ____.

    a. atomic mass   **c.** radioactivity
    b. density   **d.** atomic number

4. _____ Within the *p*-block element group, the elements at the top of the table ____ than those at the bottom.

    a. have larger radii
    b. are more metallic
    c. have lower ionization energies
    d. are less metallic

5. _____ Within a group of elements, as the atomic number increases, the atomic radius ____.

    a. generally increases
    b. remains generally constant
    c. decreases regularly
    d. decreases, but not regularly

6. _____ For each successive electron removed from an atom, the ionization energy ____.

    a. increases   **c.** remains the same
    b. decreases   **d.** shows no pattern

7. _____ The most characteristic property of the noble gases is that they are ____.

    a. metallic   **c.** metalloids
    b. radioactive   **d.** largely unreactive

8. _____ The number of valence electrons for Group 2 elements is ____.

    a. 2   **c.** 18
    b. 8   **d.** equal to the period number

FILL IN THE BLANK Write the correct term or number in the space provided.

9. The elements with atomic numbers from 57 through 71 in the periodic table are called the

_____.

10. Since the first energy level contains only the $1s$ sublevel, the number of elements in this period is

_____.

11. The electron configuration of an element is $[Ar]3d^{10}4s^24p^5$. This element is in the

_____ period.

12. Elements whose atoms contain partially filled d sublevels are called

_____.

13. For elements in Groups 1, 2, and 18, the increase in atomic number for successive elements follows

the pattern 8, 8, 18, 18, _____.

14. The electrons available to be gained, lost, or shared in the formation of chemical compounds are

called _____.

15. The energy change when an electron is acquired by a neutral atom is called the

_____ of the atom.

16. The measure of the ability of an atom in a chemical compound to attract electrons is called

_____.

17. The energy required to remove an electron from an atom is called its

_____.

18. The valence electron configuration for the Group 16 element in the third period is

_____.

19. One-half the distance between the nuclei of identical atoms that are bonded together is the

_____.

20. An atom or group of atoms that has a positive or negative charge is called a(n)

_____.

SHORT ANSWER   Write the answers to the following questions in the space provided.

21. List the group, period, and block in which the element with the electron configuration $[Rn]7s^1$ is located.

_____

22. How do the properties of the transition elements compare with those of the alkali and the alkaline-earth metals?

_____

_____

_____

23. Of the following elements, which has the largest atomic radius: sodium (atomic number 11), magnesium (atomic number 12), phosphorus (atomic number 15), and chlorine (atomic number 17). Explain your answer in terms of trends in the periodic table.

_____

_____

_____

24. Describe the general trends in ionization energies down a group and across a period.

_____

_____

25. Why are elements with high electron affinities also the most electronegative?

_____

_____

_____

_____

26. State the periodic law.

_____

_____

27. How do the sizes of a cation and an anion compare with the size of the neutral atoms from which they are formed?

_____

_____

_____

CHAPTER 5 TEST continued

MATCHING On the line at the left of each term in the first column, write the letter of the expression in the second column that is most closely related.

28. _____ main group elements

a. Group 1 elements

29. _____ lanthanides and actinides

b. elements that make up the f block

30. _____ transition elements

c. elements of the s and p blocks

31. _____ alkali metals

d. Group 17 elements

32. _____ halogens

e. entire set of d block elements

In the space provided, identify the period and block to which each of the following elements belongs.

33. Strontium: $1s^2 2s^2 2p^6 3s^2 3p^6 3d^{10} 4s^2 4p^6 5s^2$ _____

34. Krypton: $1s^2 2s^2 2p^6 3s^2 3p^6 3d^{10} 4s^2 4p^6$ _____

35. Chromium: $1s^2 2s^2 2p^6 3s^2 3p^6 3d^5 4s^1$ _____

In the space provided, write the valence electron configuration for each of the following elements.

36. Group 7, fourth period _____

37. Group 15, third period _____

38. Group 12, sixth period _____

In the space provided, list the charge of the ion most likely to be formed from the element and the name of the noble gas with an electron configuration achieved by that formation. (The atomic numbers of the noble gases are: He, 2; Ne, 10; Ar, 18; Kr, 36; Xe, 54; and Rn, 86.)

39. lithium (atomic number 3)

_____

40. oxygen (atomic number 8)

_____

41. sulfur (atomic number 16)

_____

42. aluminum (atomic number 13)

_____

CHAPTER 6 TEST
Chemical Bonding

MULTIPLE CHOICE On the line at the left of each statement, write the letter of the choice that best completes the statement or answers the question.

1. _____ An ionic bond results from electrical attraction between large numbers of ____.

    a. cations and anions   **c.** dipoles

    b. atoms   **d.** orbitals

2. _____ A nonpolar covalent bond is unlikely when two different atoms join because the atoms are likely to differ in ____.

    a. density   **c.** electronegativity

    b. state of matter   **d.** polarity

3. _____ Bond length is the distance between two bonded atoms at ____.

    a. their minimum potential energy

    b. their maximum kinetic energy

    c. their maximum potential energy

    d. one-half the diameter of the electron cloud

4. _____ To draw a Lewis structure, it is NOT necessary to know ____.

    a. which atoms are in the molecule

    b. bond energies

    c. the number of valence electrons for each atom

    d. the number of atoms in the molecule

5. _____ Multiple covalent bonds may form in molecules that contain carbon, nitrogen, or ____.

    a. chlorine   **c.** oxygen

    b. hydrogen   **d.** helium

6. _____ The principle that states that atoms tend to form compounds in which each atom has eight electrons in its highest occupied energy level is called the ____.

    a. rule of eights   **c.** Avogadro principle

    b. configuration rule   **d.** octet rule

7. _____ An example of a molecule that cannot be represented adequately by a single Lewis structure is ____.

    a. O_2 **c.** O_3

    b. CO_2 **d.** N_2

8. _____ Lattice energy is an indication of the ____.

    a. strength of an ionic bond

    b. number of ions in a crystal

    c. strength of a metallic bond

    d. strength of a covalent bond

FILL IN THE BLANK Write the correct term (or terms) in the space provided.

9. A covalent bond in which the bonded atoms have an unequal attraction for the shared electrons is

called a(n) _____.

10. A molecule containing two atoms is called a(n) _____.

11. The degree to which bonding between atoms of two elements is ionic or covalent can be

determined from the differences in the _____ of the elements.

12. A neutral group of atoms held together by covalent bonds is called a(n)

_____.

13. The electron-dot notation for a hydrogen atom is _____.

14. A shorthand representation of the composition of a substance using atomic symbols and numerical

subscripts is called a(n) _____.

15. A charged group of covalently bonded atoms is called a(n)

_____.

16. A covalent bond between two atoms produced by sharing two pairs of electrons is called

a(n) _____.

17. The simplest collection of atoms from which the formula of an ionic compound can be established

is called a(n) _____.

18. The energy required to break a chemical bond and form neutral isolated atoms is called

_____.

19. A chemical bond that results from the attraction between metal atoms and the surrounding sea of

electrons is called a(n) _____.

20. The property of being able to be drawn, pulled, or extruded through a small opening to produce a

wire is called _____.

Use VESPR theory to predict the molecular shape of the following molecules.

21. _____ carbon dioxide (CO_2)

22. _____ methane (CH_4)

23. _____ sulfur hexafluoride (SF_6)

MODERN CHEMISTRY

CHAPTER 6 TEST continued

Draw the Lewis structures for the following substances in the space provided.

24. nitrogen molecule, N_2

25. hydrogen chloride, HCl

26. carbon tetraiodide, CI_4

27. water molecule, H_2O

SHORT ANSWER   Write the answers to the following questions in the space provided.

28. Explain the intermolecular force that contributes to the high boiling point of water.

_____

_____

_____

29. What is meant by sp^3 hybridization?

_____

_____

_____

30. Compare and contrast ionic bonding and covalent bonding.

_____

_____

_____

31. Why do most atoms form chemical bonds?

_____

_____

_____

32. Compound A has a higher melting point and boiling point than compound B. At the same temperature, compound B vaporizes faster than compound A. Which of these compounds would you expect to be ionic? Why?

_____

_____

_____

33. Explain why most metals are malleable and ductile but ionic crystals are not.

_____

_____

_____

34. Explain why some molecules are best represented by resonance structures, and how these structures indicate the actual structure of the molecule.

_____

_____

_____

Use the diagram and the table below to classify the bond for each listed substance as *ionic, covalent,* **or** *polar-covalent.* **Write your answers in the space provided.**

Percent ionic character	100%	50%	5%	0%
Difference in electronegativity	3.3	1.7	0.3	0.0

Ionic   Polar covalent   Nonpolar covalent

35. F_2 _____

36. NaF _____

37. MgO _____

38. CO _____

39. $CaCl_2$ _____

40. CCl_4 _____

ELECTRONEGATIVITY VALUES

Substance	Value
Calcium (Ca)	1.0
Carbon (C)	2.5
Chlorine (Cl)	3.0
Fluorine (F)	4.0
Magnesium (Mg)	1.2
Oxygen (O)	3.5
Sodium (Na)	0.9

CHAPTER 7 TEST
Chemical Formulas and Chemical Compounds

MULTIPLE CHOICE On the line at the left of each statement, write the letter of the choice that best completes the statement or answers the question.

1. _____ Changing a subscript in a correctly written chemical formula will ____.

    a. change the number of moles represented by the formula
    b. change the charges on the other ions in the compound
    c. change the formula so that it no longer represents the same compound
    d. have no effect on the formula

2. _____ Using the stock system of nomenclature, $Cr_2(SO_4)_3$ is named ____.

    a. chromium(II) sulfate
    b. chromic sulfate
    c. dichromium trisulfate
    d. chromium(III) sulfate

3. _____ In a polyatomic ion, the algebraic sum of the oxidation numbers of all atoms is equal to ____.

    a. 0   **c.** the number of atoms in the ion
    b. 10   **d.** the charge on the ion

4. _____ The sum of the atomic masses of all the atoms in the formula for a compound would most properly be called the ____.

    a. molecular mass   **c.** atomic mass
    b. formula mass   **d.** actual mass

5. _____ The empirical formula may not represent the actual composition of a(n) ____.

    a. ionic compound   **c.** salt
    b. crystal   **d.** molecular compound

6. _____ The formula for phosphoric acid is ____.

    a. HPO_4 **c.** H_2PO_3
    b. $H(PO_4)_2$ **d.** H_3PO_4

7. _____ The term *formula mass* can be applied to both ionic compounds and molecular compounds because ____.

    a. ionic compounds exist as individual molecules
    b. molecular formulas are not always empirical formulas
    c. not all formulas represent individual molecules
    d. molecular formulas are always Lewis formulas

8. _____ To determine the correct molecular formula from an empirical formula, one must determine the ____ of the compound.

    a. density   **c.** structural formula
    b. formula mass   **d.** crystal lattice

CHAPTER 7 TEST continued

FILL IN THE BLANK   Write the oxidation number for the given element in the space provided.

9. The oxidation number of sulfur in H_2SO_4 is   _____.

10. The oxidation number of oxygen in peroxides is   _____.

11. The oxidation number of magnesium in MgO is   _____.

12. The oxidation number of silicon in $SiCl_4$ is   _____.

Write the formulas for the following compounds in the space provided.

13. silicon dioxide   _____

14. carbon tetraiodide   _____

15. tin(IV) chromate   _____

16. barium hydroxide   _____

Write the names of the following compounds in the space provided. Use the stock system or prefixes, as indicated.

17. PI_3, stock system   _____

18. N_2O_4, prefixes   _____

19. $Fe(NO_2)_2$, stock system   _____

20. CCl_4, prefixes   _____

21. CO, prefixes   _____

22. $CuCO_3$, stock system   _____

Write the formulas and give the names of the compounds formed by the following ions in the space provided.

23. Ca^{2+} and Cl^- _____

24. Pb^{2+} and CrO_4^{2-} _____

25. Al^{3+} and SO_4^{2-} _____

26. Sn^{4+} and PO_4^{3-} _____

Name each of the following ions in the space provided.

27. CN^- _____

28. O^{2-} _____

29. OH^- _____

Write the formulas and indicate the charges for the following ions in the space provided.

30. sulfide ion _____

31. copper(I) ion _____

32. carbonate ion _____

Assign oxidation numbers to each atom in the following compounds or ions. Write the oxidation numbers in the space provided.

33. H_2O_2 _____

34. CO_3^{2-} _____

35. NH_4^+ _____

PROBLEMS Use the table of atomic masses to answer the following questions. Write your answer on the line to the left, and show your work in the space provided.

Element	Symbol	Atomic mass	Element	Symbol	Atomic mass
Aluminum	Al	26.98 amu	Lead	Pb	207.2 amu
Bromine	Br	79.90 amu	Lithium	Li	6.94 amu
Carbon	C	12.01 amu	Magnesium	Mg	24.30 amu
Chlorine	Cl	35.45 amu	Manganese	Mn	54.94 amu
Chromium	Cr	52.00 amu	Nitrogen	N	14.01 amu
Copper	Cu	63.55 amu	Oxygen	O	16.00 amu
Fluorine	F	19.00 amu	Sodium	Na	22.99 amu
Hydrogen	H	1.01 amu	Sulfur	S	32.07 amu

36. _____ What is the molar mass of tetraethyl lead, $Pb(C_2H_5)_4$?

CHAPTER 7 TEST continued

37. ————————— What is the formula mass of copper(II) chloride, $CuCl_2$?

38. ————————— What is the percentage composition of $CuCl_2$ by mass?

39. ————————— Determine the mass of 0.240 mol glucose, $C_6H_{12}O_6$.

40. ————————— A sample of a compound contains 259.2 g F and 40.8 g C. Find the empirical formula.

41. ————————— The empirical formula of a compound is C_2H_5 and its formula mass is 58 amu. What is the molecular formula?

42. ————————— A sample of a compound is 80% carbon and 20% hydrogen by mass. Its formula mass is 30 amu. What is the molecular formula?

MODERN CHEMISTRY

Name _____ Date _____ Class _____

CHAPTER 8 TEST
Chemical Equations and Reactions

MULTIPLE CHOICE On the line at the left of each statement, write the letter of the choice that best completes the statement or answers the question.

1. _____ The production of a slightly soluble solid compound in a double displacement reaction results in the formation of a _____.

    a. gas   **c.** combustion reaction
    b. precipitate   **d.** halogen

2. _____ To balance a chemical equation, it is permissible to adjust the _____.

    a. coefficients   **c.** formulas of the products
    b. subscripts   **d.** number of products

3. _____ In a chemical equation, the symbol (*aq*) indicates that the substance is _____.

    a. water   **c.** an acid
    b. dissolved in water   **d.** insoluble

4. _____ The tendency for a replacement reaction to occur increases as the _____.

    a. interval between any two elements in the activity series decreases
    b. temperature decreases
    c. valence electrons are used up
    d. interval between any two elements in the activity series increases

5. _____ The coefficients in a chemical equation _____.

    a. indicate the number of moles of each substance that react
    b. show the number of grams of each substance that react
    c. are the molar masses of the substances
    d. show the valence electrons for each atom

6. _____ If metal X is lower than metal Y in the activity series, then _____.

    a. X will replace ions of Y in solution
    b. Y will replace ions of X in solution
    c. Y will form oxides only indirectly
    d. X will react with cold water

7. _____ In a reaction, the ions of two compounds exchange places in aqueous solution to form two new compounds. This reaction is called a(n) _____.

    a. synthesis reaction
    b. decomposition reaction
    c. single-replacement reaction
    d. double-replacement reaction

8. _____ The use of a double arrow in a chemical equation indicates that the reaction _____.

    a. is reversible   **c.** is written backward
    b. requires heat   **d.** has not been confirmed in the laboratory

FILL IN THE BLANK **Write the correct term (or terms) in the space provided.**

9. A small whole number that appears in front of a formula in a chemical equation is called

a(n) _____.

10. In a chemical equation, the symbol (l) indicates that the substance is

_____.

11. A chemical reaction in which the products re-form the original reactants is

a(n) _____.

12. The general equation for a synthesis reaction is _____.

13. The general equation for a decomposition reaction is _____.

14. The general equation for a single-replacement reaction is _____.

15. The general equation for a double-replacement reaction is _____.

16. Oxides of active metals, such as CaO, react with water to form

_____.

17. A chemical reaction in which a substance combines with oxygen, releasing a large amount of

energy as heat and light, is a(n) _____.

18. The decomposition of a substance by an electric current is called

_____.

19. A list of elements ordered by the ease with which they undergo certain chemical reactions is

a(n) _____.

20. The names and relative amounts of reactants and products in a chemical reaction are represented

using symbols and formulas in a(n) _____.

21. The law of _____ must be satisfied for a chemical equation to be
balanced.

22. A(n) _____ product is sometimes indicated by an arrow pointing
upward.

23. The symbol $\xrightarrow{\Delta}$ means that the reactants are _____.

CHAPTER 8 TEST continued

SHORT ANSWER Write the answers to the following questions in the space provided.

24. How are a word equation and a formula equation alike? How do they differ from a chemical equation?

_____

_____

_____

25. What are three observations that indicate a chemical change may be taking place?

_____

_____

_____

Write a word equation for each chemical reaction in the space provided.

26. $2ZnS(s) + 3O_2(g) \rightarrow 2ZnO(s) + 2SO_2(g)$

_____

27. $2NaI + Cl_2 \rightarrow 2NaCl + I_2$

_____

Write a formula equation for each word equation in the space provided.

28. magnesium + oxygen $\rightarrow$ magnesium oxide

_____

29. calcium carbonate $\rightarrow$ calcium oxide + carbon dioxide

_____

On the line to the left, identify each equation as a *synthesis, decomposition, single-replacement,* **or** *double-replacement* **reaction.**

30. _____ $2H_2O(l) \rightarrow 2H_2(g) + O_2(g)$

31. _____ $Cl_2(g) + 2KBr(aq) \rightarrow 2KCl(aq) + Br_2(l)$

32. _____ $CaO(s) + H_2O(l) \rightarrow Ca(OH)_2(s)$

33. _____ $HCl(aq) + NaOH(aq) \rightarrow NaCl(aq) + H_2O(l)$

Balance the following equations in the space provided.

34. $AgNO_3 + CuCl_2 \rightarrow AgCl + Cu(NO_3)_2$

_____

35. $PbO_2 \rightarrow PbO + O_2$

_____

36. $Zn(OH)_2 + CH_3COOH \rightarrow Zn(CH_3COO)_2 + H_2O$

_____

Using the activity series table, predict whether each of the following reactions will occur. Write _no reaction_ for those that will not occur. For the reactions that will occur, write the products and balance the equation in the space provided.

Activity Series of the Elements

Metals		Halogens
Li	React with cold	F_2
Rb	H_2O and acids, replacing	Cl_2
K	hydrogen. React	Br_2
Ba	with oxygen	I_2
Sr	forming acids.	
Ca		
Na		
Mg	React with steam	
Al	(but not cold H_2O)	
Mn	and acids, replacing	
Zn	hydrogen. React	
Cr	with oxygen,	
Fe	forming oxides.	
Cd		
Co	Do not react with water.	
Ni	React with acids, replacing	
Sn	hydrogen. React with	
Pb	oxygen, forming acids.	
H_2	React with oxygen,	
Sb	forming oxides.	
Bi		
Cu		
Hg		
Ag	Fairly unreactive,	
Pt	forming oxides only	
Au	indirectly.	

37. $Mg(s) + \text{steam} \rightarrow$ _____

_____

38. $Pt(s) + O_2(g) \rightarrow$ _____

_____

39. $Cl_2(g) + MgBr_2(aq) \rightarrow$ _____

_____

40. $Zn(s) + HCl(aq) \rightarrow$ _____

_____

41. $Cr(s) + H_2O(l) \rightarrow$ _____

_____

42. $Ni(s) + CuCl_2(aq) \rightarrow$ _____

_____

43. $Ni(s) + H_2O(l) \rightarrow$ _____

_____

44. $Mg(s) + Co(NO_3)_2(aq) \rightarrow$ _____

_____

CHAPTER 9 TEST
Stoichiometry

MULTIPLE CHOICE On the line at the left of each statement, write the letter of the choice that best completes the statement or answers the question.

1. _____ Knowing the mole ratio of a reactant and product in a chemical reaction would allow you to determine _____.

  a. the energy released in the reaction
  b. the speed of the reaction
  c. the mass of the product produced from a known mass of reactant
  d. whether the reaction was reversible

2. _____ In the reaction $6CO_2 + 6H_2O \rightarrow C_6H_{12}O_6 + 6O_2$, the mole ratio of water to oxygen is _____.

  a. 2:1   **c.** 3:2
  b. 1:1   **d.** 6:8

3. _____ In the reaction $Al_2(SO_4)_3 + 3Ca(OH)_2 \rightarrow 3CaSO_4 + 2Al(OH)_3$, the mole ratio of calcium hydroxide to aluminum hydroxide is _____.

  a. 1:3   **c.** 1:1
  b. 2:3   **d.** 3:2

4. _____ For the reaction $N_2 + 3H_2 \rightarrow 2NH_3$, how many moles of nitrogen are required to produce 18 mol of ammonia?

  a. 9   **c.** 27
  b. 18   **d.** 36

5. _____ In the reaction $A + B \rightarrow C + D$, if there is more reactant B than is required to completely react with all of A, then _____.

  a. A is the limiting reactant   **c.** there is no limiting reactant
  b. B is the limiting reactant   **d.** no product can be formed

6. _____ If a chemist *calculates* the maximum amount of product that could be obtained in a chemical reaction, he or she is calculating the _____.

  a. theoretical yield   **c.** mole ratio
  b. percent yield   **d.** actual yield

7. _____ The actual yield of a chemical reaction is _____.

  a. less than the theoretical yield
  b. greater than the theoretical yield
  c. equal to the percent yield
  d. greater than the percent yield

8. _____ Fewer steps are required to solve stoichiometry problems when the reactant is given in _____ and the product is sought in _____.

  a. grams, grams   **c.** grams, liters
  b. moles, moles   **d.** liters, number of atoms

CHAPTER 9 TEST continued

FILL IN THE BLANK For each example, list the *given* and *unknown* information.

9. given: _____

unknown: _____

For the reaction $N_2 + 3H_2 \rightarrow 2NH_3$, a chemist must determine how many grams of nitrogen are needed to produce 500 g of ammonia.

10. given: _____

unknown: _____

A chemist must determine how many moles of H_2 can be produced from 500 g of H_2O in the reaction $2Na + 2H_2O \rightarrow 2NaOH + H_2$.

11. given: _____

unknown: _____

A chemist must determine how many grams of carbon monoxide are needed to produce 20 mol of CO_2 in the reaction $2CO + O_2 \rightarrow 2CO_2$.

12. given: _____

unknown: _____

In the reaction $2H_2O \rightarrow 2H_2 + O_2$, a chemist must determine how many moles of oxygen can be produced from 50 mol of water.

13. given: _____

unknown: _____

A chemist must determine how many grams of sulfur are required to produce 800 g of sulfur dioxide using the equation $S + O_2 \rightarrow SO_2$.

Write the correct equation or term in the space provided.

14. Give the correct mathematical expression for determining percent yield.

Percent yield = _____

15. Fill in the steps necessary to find the number of grams of substance B produced from the number of grams of substance A.

grams of A $\rightarrow$ _____ $\rightarrow$ _____ $\rightarrow$ grams of B

16. The conversion factor for deriving the number of moles of salicylic acid, $C_7H_6O_3$, from a given

number of grams of salicylic acid is _____.

17. The substance that restricts the amount of other reactants used in a chemical reaction is known

as the _____.

18. The measured amount of product obtained from a chemical reaction is called the

_____.

19. The substance that is not completely used up in a chemical reaction is known as the

_____.

20. If the theoretical yield for a chemical reaction is 100. g and the percent yield is 70.0%, the actual

yield is _____.

CHAPTER 9 TEST continued

PROBLEMS Write the answers to the questions on the line to the left, and show your work in the space provided.

Element	Symbol	Atomic Mass	Element	Symbol	Atomic Mass
Bromine	Br	79.90 amu	Lead	Pb	207.2 amu
Carbon	C	12.01 amu	Nitrogen	N	14.01 amu
Chlorine	Cl	35.45 amu	Oxygen	O	16.00 amu
Hydrogen	H	1.01 amu	Potassium	K	39.10 amu
Iodine	I	126.90 amu	Sodium	Na	22.99 amu
Iron	Fe	55.85 amu	Sulfur	S	32.07 amu

21. _____ For the reaction $2Fe + O_2 \rightarrow 2FeO$, how many grams of iron oxide will be produced from 8.00 mol of iron?

22. _____ If cyclohexanol is burned as a fuel in the following reaction, how many moles of oxygen are needed to produce 13.7 mol of carbon dioxide?
$2C_6H_{12}O + 17O_2 \rightarrow 12CO_2 + 12H_2O$

23. _____ For the reaction $Pb(NO_3)_2 + 2KI \rightarrow PbI_2 + 2KNO_3$, how many moles of lead iodide are produced from 300. g of potassium iodide?

24. _____ For the reaction $2KClO_3 \rightarrow 2KCl + 3O_2$, how many grams of potassium chlorate are required to produce 160. g of oxygen?

25. _____ How many grams of carbon dioxide are produced from the combustion of 250. g of ethane, C_3H_8, in the reaction $C_3H_8 + 5O_2 \rightarrow 3CO_2 + 4H_2O$?

26. _____ In the reaction $2Na + 2H_2O \rightarrow 2NaOH + H_2$, how many grams of hydrogen are produced if 120. g of Na and 80.0 g of H_2O are available?

27. _____ Calculate the percent yield for the reaction $CH_4 + 2O_2 \rightarrow 2H_2O + CO_2$, when 1000. g of CH_4 react with excess O_2 to produce 2300. g of CO_2.

Use the reaction $Cl_2 + 2KBr \rightarrow 2KCl + Br_2$ for problems 28–30.

28. _____ How many moles of potassium chloride are produced from 119 g of potassium bromide?

29. _____ How many grams of potassium chloride can be produced from 300. g each of Cl_2 and KBr?

30. _____ What is the percent yield if 200. g of Cl_2 react with an excess of KBr to produce 410. g of Br_2?

MODERN CHEMISTRY

Physical Characteristics of Gases

MULTIPLE CHOICE   On the line at the left of each statement, write the letter of the choice that best completes the statement or answers the question.

1. _____ A real gas _____.

    a. does not completely obey the predictions of the kinetic-molecular theory
    b. consists of particles that do not occupy space
    c. cannot be condensed
    d. does not diffuse

2. _____ According to the kinetic-molecular theory, particles of a gas _____.

    a. attract each other but do not collide
    b. repel each other and collide
    c. collide but do not attract or repel each other
    d. do not collide and do not attract or repel each other

3. _____ Diffusion between two gases occurs most rapidly if the two gases are at a _____.

    a. high temperature and the molecules are small
    b. low temperature and the molecules are large
    c. low temperature and the molecules are small
    d. high temperature and the molecules are large

4. _____ The kinetic-molecular theory does not work well for _____.

    a. any real gases   **c.** gases at very low temperatures
    b. gases at low pressure   **d.** real gases at high temperatures

5. _____ If the temperature of a gas remains constant, then the pressure of the gas will increase if _____.

    a. the mass of the gas molecules decreases
    b. the diffusion of the gas molecules increases
    c. the size of the container is decreased
    d. the number of gas molecules in the container is decreased

6. _____ According to the equation $KE = \frac{1}{2}mv^2$, hydrogen molecules have _____ than heavier oxygen molecules at the same temperature.

    a. less kinetic energy   **c.** higher average speeds
    b. more kinetic energy   **d.** lower average speeds

7. _____ The gas most likely to deviate from ideal gas behavior is _____.

    a. NH_3 **c.** He
    b. H_2 **d.** O_2

FILL IN THE BLANK   Write the correct term (or terms) in the space provided.

8. If a fixed quantity and volume of a gas undergoes a change in temperature, it will also experience a

change in _____.

9. To study the relationship between the pressure and volume of a gas, hold the

_____ constant.

10. Standard pressure is the atmospheric pressure balanced by a column of mercury whose height is

exactly _____.

11. If the temperature remains constant for a gas, V and P represent the original volume and pressure, and V' and P' represent the new volume and pressure, the mathematical expression for Boyle's law

is _____.

12. _____ describes the properties of solids, liquids, and gases in terms of the motion of particles.

13. The process by which gas particles under pressure flow through a tiny opening is called

_____.

14. An imaginary gas that conforms perfectly to all of the predictions of the kinetic-molecular theory is

called a(n) _____.

15. The spontaneous mixing of the particles of two substances caused by their random motion is called

_____.

16. The force per unit area on a surface is called _____.

17. The SI unit of force is the _____.

18. A device used to measure atmospheric pressure is a(n) _____.

19. The pressure exerted by each gas in a mixture is called the _____ of that gas.

20. If the temperature and number of moles of a gas remain constant, but the volume increases, the

pressure of the gas will _____.

21. The lowest possible temperature, corresponding to zero on the Kelvin scale, is referred to as

_____.

22. If no kinetic energy is lost, a collision is called _____.

23. Because liquids and gases flow, they are called _____.

CHAPTER 10 TEST continued

MATCHING On the line to the left of each expression in the first column, write the letter of the expression in the second column that is most closely related.

24. _____ The pressure of a fixed mass of gas varies directly with the Kelvin temperature at constant volume.

25. _____ The volume of a fixed mass of gas varies inversely with the pressure at constant temperature.

26. _____ The total pressure of a mixture of gases is equal to the sum of the partial pressures of the component gases.

27. _____ The relationship between pressure, volume, and temperature is expressed by this law.

28. _____ The volume of a fixed mass of gas varies directly with the Kelvin temperature at constant pressure.

a. Dalton's law

b. Charles's law

c. Gay-Lussac's law

d. Boyle's law

e. combined gas law

f. Pascal's law

g. gas pressure law

PROBLEMS Write the answers to the following questions on the line to the left, and show your work in the space provided.

29. _____ Convert 0.75 atm to mm Hg.

30. _____ The pressure of a sample of helium in a 200 mL container is 2.0 atm. If the helium is compressed to a volume of 10 mL without changing the temperature, what would be the pressure of the gas?

31. _____ The volume of a gas at 7.0°C is 49 mL. If the volume increases to 74 mL and the pressure is constant, what will the temperature of the gas be?

32. _____ A sample of gas occupies 1000. mL at standard pressure. What volume will the gas occupy at a pressure of 800. mm Hg if the temperature remains constant?

33. _____ The pressure of a 1000. mL sample of gas is 700. mm Hg and its temperature is 10.°C. If the volume is constant, what will the temperature be at 900. mm Hg?

34. _____ If five gases in a cylinder each exert a partial pressure of 2.50 atm, what is the total pressure exerted by the gases?

35. _____ The pressure of a 70.0 L sample of gas is 600. mm Hg at 20.0°C. If the temperature drops to 15.0°C and the volume expands to 90.0 L, what will the pressure of the gas be?

36. _____ The pressure of a sample of gas at constant volume is 8.0 atm at 70.°C. What will the pressure be at 20.°C?

37. _____ The volume of a gas is 120. L at 0.500 atm and 15.0°C. What volume will it occupy at 0.250 atm and 10.0°C?

38. _____ The volume of a gas is 400. mL at 30.0°C. What volume will it occupy at 50.0°C if the pressure remains constant?

Name _____ Date _____ Class _____

Molecular Composition of Gases

MULTIPLE CHOICE On the line at the left of each statement, write the letter of the choice that best completes the statement or answers the question.

1. _____ When Gay-Lussac's law of combining volumes holds, which of the following can be expressed in ratios of small whole numbers?

   a. pressures before and after reaction
   b. volumes of gaseous reactants and products
   c. Kelvin temperatures
   d. molar masses of products and molar masses of reactants

2. _____ Equal volumes of ideal gases at the same temperature and pressure contain equal numbers of _____.

   a. protons   **c.** particles
   b. ions   **d.** Dalton's ultimate particles

3. _____ At constant temperature and pressure, the volume of a gas is directly proportional to its _____.

   a. molar mass   **c.** density at STP
   b. number of moles   **d.** rate of diffusion

4. _____ The value of the gas constant is _____.

   a. 0.0821 L·atm/mol·K   **c.** 0.0281 L·atm/mol·K
   b. 0.0281 L·atm   **d.** 0.0821 mol·K

5. _____ To use the ideal gas law to determine the molar mass of a gas, _____.

   a. the mass of a molar volume of that gas must be determined
   b. the mass of any known volume of the gas may be used
   c. a volume of less than 22.4 L may not be used
   d. the volume measurement must be made at STP

6. _____ Suppose that two unlike gases are injected into opposite ends of a long tube at the same time and allowed to diffuse toward the center. They should begin to mix _____.

   a. at the end that held the heavier gas
   b. closer to the end where the heavier gas entered
   c. closer to the end where the lighter gas entered
   d. exactly in the middle

7. _____ All elements that are gases near room temperature, except the noble gases, normally exist as _____.

   a. monatomic molecules   **c.** positive ions
   b. negative ions   **d.** diatomic molecules

FILL IN THE BLANK Write the correct equation or term (or terms) in the space provided.

8. In the equation $N_2(g) + 3H_2(g) \rightarrow 2NH_3(g)$, one volume of N_2 yields

_____ volumes of NH_3.

9. The volume occupied by 1 mol of oxygen at STP is _____.

10. The process by which gas molecules confined in a container pass through a small opening in the

container is called _____.

11. The ideal gas law combines Boyle's law, Charles's law and _____.

12. The ideal gas law is $PV =$ _____.

13. When the ideal gas law reduces to $PV = k$, the expression is equivalent to

_____ law.

14. In the equation $N_2(g) + 2O_2(g) \rightarrow 2NO_2(g)$, the volume ratio of N_2 to NO_2 is

_____.

15. The pressure of a gas is directly proportional to the number of moles if both volume and

_____ are constant.

MATCHING On the line to the left of each expression in the first column, write the letter of the expression in the second column that is most closely related.

16. _____ At constant temperature and pressure, the volumes of gaseous reactants and products can be expressed as ratios of small whole numbers.

17. _____ Equal volumes of gases at the same temperature and pressure contain equal numbers of molecules.

18. _____ Pressure times volume equals molar amount times 0.0821 L·atm/mol·K.

19. _____ The rates of effusion of gases at the same temperature and pressure are inversely proportional to their molar masses.

20. _____ Volume divided by temperature equals a constant when molar amount and pressure are constant.

a. ideal gas law

b. Charles's law

c. Gay-Lussac's law of combining volumes

d. Boyle's law

e. Avogadro's law

f. Graham's law

CHAPTER 11 TEST continued

PROBLEMS Write the answers to the following questions on the line to the left, and show your work in the space provided.

21. _____ When hydrogen burns, water vapor is produced according to the unbalanced equation $H_2(g) + O_2(g) \rightarrow H_2O(g)$. If 12 L of oxygen are consumed, what volume of water vapor is produced?

22. _____ What is the volume of 24.0 g of oxygen gas (32.00 g/mol) at STP?

23. _____ The mass of a 1.0 L sample of a gas is 0.716 g at STP. What is the molar mass of the gas?

24. _____ What is the density at STP of NO_2 gas (46.01 g/mol) in grams per liter?

25. _____ What is the mass of 10.0 L of chlorine gas (70.90 g/mol) at 27°C and 3.50 atm?

26. _____ What is the volume of 2.0 g of CS_2 vapor (76.15 g/mol) at 70.°C and 726 mm Hg?

27. _____ What pressure (in atm) is exerted by 0.750 mol of a gas in a 5.00 L container at 0.00°C?

28. _____ A 200. mL sample of gas is collected at 20.0°C and 733.5 mm Hg. The mass of the sample is 0.934 g. What is the molar mass of the gas?

29. _____ Assuming all volume measurements are made at the same temperature and pressure, what volume of hydrogen gas is needed to react completely with 6.55 L of oxygen gas to produce water vapor?

30. _____ When calcium carbonate is heated, it produces calcium oxide and carbon dioxide. The equation for the reaction is $CaCO_3(s) \rightarrow CaO(s) + CO_2(g)$. How many grams of calcium carbonate (100.09 g/mol) must be decomposed to produce 5.00 L of carbon dioxide at STP?

31. _____ How many times greater is the rate of effusion of fluorine gas, F_2 (38.00 g/mol), than that of bromine gas, Br_2 (159.80 g/mol), at the same temperature and pressure?

32. _____ A quantity of chlorine gas (70.90 g/mol) occupies a volume of 50.0 L at 27.0°C and 721 mm Hg. What is the mass of the chlorine?

CHAPTER 12 TEST
Liquids and Solids

MULTIPLE CHOICE   On the line at the left of each statement, write the letter of the choice that best completes the statement or answers the question.

1. _____ Liquids diffuse more slowly than gases because _____.

   a. liquids cannot be compressed
   b. the attractive forces between particles impede their movement
   c. the particles in a liquid are not mobile
   d. liquids are always at lower temperatures than gases

2. _____ When heated, a pure crystalline solid will _____.

   a. gradually soften before it melts
   b. melt over a wide temperature range
   c. exhibit a sharply defined melting temperature
   d. melt at a temperature slightly above its freezing temperature

3. _____ A system is at equilibrium when _____.

   a. no physical or chemical changes are occurring
   b. the physical changes counteract the chemical changes
   c. opposing physical or chemical changes occur at equal rates
   d. only physical changes are occurring

4. _____ Solids have all of the following properties except _____.

   a. definite shape   **c.** high density
   b. fluidity   **d.** definite volume

5. _____ When heat is applied to a liquid-vapor system at equilibrium, a new equilibrium state will have _____.

   a. a higher percentage of liquid   **c.** equal amounts of liquid and vapor
   b. a higher percentage of vapor   **d.** all liquid

6. _____ At the same temperature, different liquids will have different equilibrium vapor pressures because _____.

   a. the energy of the particles is the same for different liquids
   b. diffusions rates differ for the liquids
   c. the attractive forces between the particles in the liquids differ
   d. they cannot all be at equilibrium at once

7. _____ If water molecules were nonpolar, water would probably _____.

   a. be a solid at room temperature   **c.** be a gas at room temperature
   b. have stronger hydrogen bonding   **d.** be flammable

8. _____ As atmospheric pressure on the surface of a liquid decreases, its boiling point _____.

   a. decreases   **c.** remains unchanged
   b. increases   **d.** shows no correlation

FILL IN THE BLANK Write the correct term (or terms) in the space provided.

9. The temperature above which a substance cannot exist in the liquid state is its

_____.

10. The force that tends to pull a liquid's surface together and minimize its surface area is

_____.

11. Particles are arranged randomly in a(n) _____ solid.

12. The pressure exerted by a vapor in equilibrium with its corresponding liquid at a given temperature

is its _____.

13. The temperature and pressure at which the solid, liquid, and vapor of a substance can coexist at

equilibrium is the _____.

14. The heat required to melt 1 mol of a solid at its melting point is its

_____.

15. The smallest portion of a crystal lattice that shows the three-dimensional pattern of the entire

lattice is its _____.

16. _____ crystals conduct electricity because valence electrons are
free to move throughout the crystal lattice.

MATCHING Match the letter on the diagram with the term for that point or region.

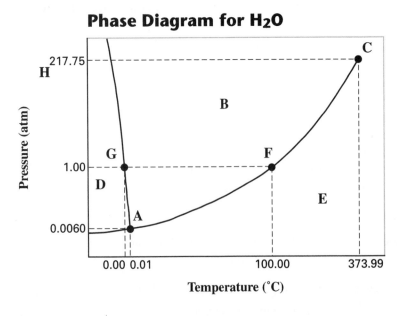

Phase Diagram for H₂O

17. _____ Critical point

18. _____ Vapor

19. _____ Normal freezing point

20. _____ Triple point

21. _____ Solid

22. _____ Normal boiling point

23. _____ Liquid

24. _____ Critical pressure

MODERN CHEMISTRY

SHORT ANSWER   Write the answers to the following questions in the space provided.

25. Use the kinetic-molecular theory to explain why liquids are fluids, how liquids diffuse, and why they evaporate.

_____

_____

_____

_____

_____

26. Distinguish between ionic crystals and metallic crystals.

_____

_____

_____

_____

_____

27. Using the term *equilibrium vapor pressure*, explain what happens to the boiling point of water at high elevations and why this happens.

_____

_____

_____

_____

28. List three types of crystals, and state a physical property specific to each.

_____

_____

_____

29. Why does equilibrium vapor pressure increase as temperature increases?

_____

_____

_____

_____

MATCHING On the line at the left of each term in the first column, write the letter of the expression in the second column that is most closely related.

30. _____ evaporation

31. _____ boiling

32. _____ condensation

33. _____ melting

34. _____ sublimation

35. _____ vaporization

36. _____ deposition

37. _____ capillary action

a. attraction of the surface of a liquid to the surface of a solid

b. process by which a liquid or solid changes to a gas

c. change of state from a solid directly to a gas

d. process by which particles escape from the surface of a non-boiling liquid and enter the gas state

e. physical change of a liquid to a solid by the removal of heat

f. conversion of a liquid to a vapor both within the liquid and at the liquid's surface

g. physical change from a solid to a liquid by the addition of heat

h. process by which a gas changes to a liquid

i. change of state from a gas directly to a solid

PROBLEMS Write the answers to the following questions on the line to the left, and show your work in the space provided.

38. _____ The molar heat of fusion for water is 6.008 kJ/mol. How much energy would be required to melt 47.0 g of ice (18.02 g/mol)?

39. _____ Calculate the molar heat of vaporization of a substance if 0.433 mol of the substance absorbs 4.307 kJ when it melts.

40. _____ Calculate the energy released by freezing 26.6 g of a liquid. Its molar mass is 82.9 g/mol, and its molar heat of fusion is 4.60 kJ/mol.

CHAPTER 13 TEST

Solutions

MULTIPLE CHOICE On the line at the left of each statement, write the letter of the choice that best completes the statement or answers the question.

1. _____ Molecules whose water solutions conduct electric current _____.

    a. are nonpolar   **c.** do not dissolve in water

    b. ionize in water   **d.** decompose in water

2. _____ Which of the following does NOT increase the rate at which a solid dissolves in water?

    a. raising the temperature   **c.** using large pieces of the solid

    b. stirring   **d.** crushing the solid

3. _____ When the energy released by the formation of solvent-solute attractions is greater than the energy absorbed by overcoming solute-solute and solvent-solvent attractions, the dissolving process _____.

    a. has a negative heat of solution   **c.** occurs rapidly

    b. has a positive heat of solution   **d.** does not occur

4. _____ Henry's law relates _____.

    a. pressure to gas-liquid solubility

    b. temperature to gas-liquid solubility

    c. pressure to temperature

    d. pressure to liquid-solid solubility

5. _____ Raising the temperature of a solvent causes solvent-solvent collisions to become _____.

    a. less frequent and more energetic   **c.** less frequent and less energetic

    b. more frequent and more energetic   **d.** more frequent and less energetic

6. _____ Solubility of a solute depends on _____.

    a. the nature of the solute and the temperature

    b. the nature of the solute only

    c. the temperature only

    d. neither the nature of the solute nor the temperature

7. _____ Effervescence is the _____.

    a. dissolving of a gas in a liquid

    b. escape of a gas from a container of gas

    c. escape of a solid from a solid-liquid solution

    d. escape of a gas from a gas-liquid solution

8. _____ A solution that contains a high concentration of solute but than can hold even more solute is _____.

    a. unsaturated and dilute   **c.** unsaturated and concentrated

    b. saturated and dilute   **d.** saturated and concentrated

FILL IN THE BLANK   Write the correct term (or terms) in the space provided.

9. As temperature increases, the solubility of gases in liquids _____.

10. The substance dissolved in a homogeneous mixture is the _____.

11. A mixture that can be identified because it scatters light is

a(n) _____.

12. When a solute dissolves and recrystallizes at the same rate, the solution is at

_____.

13. A substance that does not dissolve in a polar solvent is probably

_____.

14. To conduct electricity, a solution must contain _____.

15. A solution that contains more dissolved solute than does a saturated solution under the same

conditions is called a(n) _____.

16. Mixtures are classified according to their _____.

17. A homogeneous mixture that contains particles in a dispersed phase that do not settle out is a(n)

_____.

18. Dissolution processes with negative heats of solution are _____
processes.

19. _____ is the solution process with water as the solvent.

20. Liquid solutes and solvents that are not soluble in each other are

_____.

21. A solute molecule that is surrounded by solvent molecules is _____.

22. $CuSO_4 \cdot 5H_2O$ is a crystalline compound referred to as a _____.

23. The solubility of $CuCl_2(s)$ would _____ with increasing
temperature.

24. A(n) _____ is a solution whose solute and solvent are both solid
metals.

SHORT ANSWER Write the answers to the following questions in the space provided.

25. Explain the meaning of the phrase "like dissolves like" in terms of polar and nonpolar substances.

_____

_____

_____

26. What are the differences between molarity and molality?

_____

_____

_____

27. Compare the properties of solutions, suspensions, and colloids.

_____

_____

_____

28. Ethanol dissolves in water, but carbon tetrachloride does not. What can you conclude about ethanol and carbon tetrachloride?

_____

_____

_____

PROBLEMS Write the answers to the following questions on the line to the left, and show your work in the space provided.

29. _____ Exactly 15.0 g of a substance can be dissolved in 150.0 g of water. What is the solubility of the substance in grams per hundred grams of water?

30. _____ What mass of water must be used to make a 1.35 m solution that contains 8.20 mol NaOH?

31. _____ The solubility of a substance is 12.0 g per 100. g of water at 20.0°C, and is 18.0 g per 100. g of water at 60.0°C. How many grams of the substance can crystallize from a saturated solution that contains 200. g of water at 60.0°C if the solution is cooled to 20.0°C?

32. _____ What mass of HNO_3 is present in 86 g of a solution that is 9.5% HNO_3 by mass?

33. _____ What mass of iodine, I_2 (molar mass, 253.80 g/mol), must be used to prepare a 0.960 m solution if 100.0 g of methanol, CH_3OH, is used?

34. _____ What is the molarity of a solution composed of 8.210 g of potassium chromate, K_2CrO_4 (molar mass, 194.20 g/mol), dissolved in enough water to make 0.500 L of solution?

35. _____ What volume of 1.50 M NaCl (molar mass, 58.44 g/mol) is needed for a reaction that requires 146.3 g of NaCl?

36. _____ What is the molal concentration of a solution made by dissolving 34.2 g of sucrose, $C_{12}H_{22}O_{11}$ (molar mass, 342.34 g/mol), in 125 g of water.

CHAPTER 14 TEST

Ions in Aqueous Solutions and Colligative Properties

MULTIPLE CHOICE On the line at the left of each statement, write the letter of the choice that best completes the statement or answers the question.

1. _____ A colligative property is one that depends on _____.

    a. the number of solute particles but not their identity
    b. the identity of solute particles but not their number
    c. both the number and the identity of solute particles
    d. neither the number nor the identity of solute particles

2. _____ Which of the following is NOT a colligative property?

    a. boiling-point elevation   **c.** freezing-point depression
    b. vapor-pressure lowering   **d.** electrical conductivity

3. _____ The right side of the incomplete hydration equilibrium equation $Li^+ + nH_2O \leftrightarrows$ should be

    a. $Li + [nH_2O]^+$ **c.** $[Li^+ \cdot (H_2O)_n]$
    b. $Li^- \cdot nH_2O^{2+}$ **d.** $[Li \cdot nH_2O]^+$

4. _____ Which ion is a spectator ion in the following equation?
$$Cu^{2+}(aq) + Zn^{2+}(aq) + 2S^{2-}(aq) \rightarrow CuS(s) + ZnS(s)$$

    a. $Cu^{2+}(aq)$ **c.** $S^{2-}(aq)$
    b. $Zn^{2+}(aq)$ **d.** none of the above

5. _____ To determine the molar mass of a solute by using colligative properties, you must know the

    _____.

    a. volume of the solution   **c.** temperature of the solution
    b. mass of the solute   **d.** volume of the solute

6. _____ The net ionic equation for the precipitation reaction between silver nitrate solution and sodium sulfide solution is _____.

    a. $2Ag^+(aq) + 2NO_3^-(aq) + 2Na^+(aq) + S^{2-}(aq) \rightarrow Ag_2S(s) + 2Na^+(aq)$
    b. $2Ag^+(aq) + S^{2-}(aq) \rightarrow Ag_2S(s)$
    c. $2Ag^+(aq) + 2NO_3^-(aq) + 2Na^+(aq) + S^{2-}(aq) \rightarrow Ag_2S(s) + 2NaNO_3(s) + S^{2-}(aq)$
    d. $2Ag^-(aq) + S^{2+}(aq) \rightarrow Ag_2S(s)$

7. _____ Which ions do not appear in the net ionic equation for the precipitation involving solutions of $Zn(NO_3)_2$ and Na_3PO_4?

    a. $Zn^{2+}(aq)$ and $NO_3^-(aq)$ **c.** $Zn^{2+}(aq)$ and $PO_4^{3-}(aq)$
    b. $Na^+(aq)$ and $Zn^{2+}(aq)$ **d.** $Na^+(aq)$ and $NO_3^-(aq)$

8. _____ Nonvolatile solutes _____.

    a. depress freezing point and elevate boiling point
    b. elevate freezing point and depress boiling point
    c. depress both freezing and boiling points
    d. elevate both freezing and boiling points

FILL IN THE BLANK Write the correct term (or terms) in the space provided.

9. When a solid is formed from the combination of two solutions of ionic compounds, it is called

_____.

10. _____ allow the movement of some particles while blocking the movement of others.

11. Any substance whose water solution conducts electricity is a(n) _____.

12. An ion that does NOT take part in a chemical reaction is called a(n)

_____.

13. The number of moles of ions produced by the dissociation of 1 mol of $MgCl_2$ is

_____.

14. _____ is the external pressure that must be applied to stop osmosis.

15. The symbol for the hydronium ion is _____.

16. The ions $Ca^{2+}(aq)$ and $NO_3^-(aq)$ are produced by the dissociation of the compound whose formula

is _____.

17. The vapor pressure of pure water is _____ than the vapor pressure for an aqueous solution.

18. The boiling point of a 1 M solution of glucose (a non-electrolyte) will be

_____ than a 1 M solution of NaCl (a strong electrolyte).

19. The right-hand side of the equation for the dissolving of K_2S is _____.

SHORT ANSWER Write the answers to the following questions in the space provided.

20. Explain how ionization and dissociation differ.

_____

_____

_____

_____

21. Distinguish between a strong electrolyte and a weak electrolyte.

_____

_____

_____

22. Why is the hydronium ion used to represent the hydrogen ion in a solution?

_____

_____

_____

23. Explain why salt is frequently added to icy roads in the winter.

_____

_____

_____

Use the guidelines below to determine which of the following combinations of solutions will produce a precipitate. If no precipitate forms, write *none.* **If a precipitate forms, write the net ionic equation for the reaction.**

General Solubility Guidelines

1. Most sodium, potassium, and ammonium compounds are soluble in water.
2. Most nitrates, acetates, and chlorates are soluble.
3. Most chlorides are soluble except those of silver, mercury(II), and lead. (Lead(II) chloride is soluble in hot water.)
4. Most sulfates are soluble except those of calcium, barium, strontium, and lead.
5. Most carbonates, phosphates, and silicates are insoluble except those of sodium, potassium, and ammonium.
6. Most sulfides are insoluble except those of calcium, strontium, sodium, potassium, and ammonium.

24. KCl and $Ca(NO_3)_2$

_____

25. Na_2SO_4 and $BaCl_2$

_____

26. $(NH_4)_2S$ and $Cd(NO_3)_2$

_____

27. NH_4Cl and Na_2SO_4

_____

28. $Ca(NO_3)_2$ and $CuCl_2$

_____

PROBLEMS Write the answers to the following questions on the line to the left, and show your work in the space provided.

29. _____ A solution with 3.11 g of a nonelectrolyte solute in 38 g of water ($K_b = 0.51°C/m$) has a boiling point elevated by 1.00°C. What is the molar mass of the solute?

30. _____ The boiling point of a solvent is elevated by 2.4°C when the solute concentration is 3.1 m. What is K_b?

31. _____ What is the freezing-point depression of a solution that contains 0.705 mol of a nonelectrolyte solute in 5.02 kg of water? ($K_f = -1.86°C/m$)

32. _____ The freezing point of a solvent is lowered by 2.89°C when the solute concentration is 1.03 m. What is K_f?

33. _____ How many grams of a nonelectrolyte solute that has a molar mass of 41.9 g/mol must be added to 1.0×10^4 g of water to raise the boiling point 0.84°C? ($K_b = 0.51°C/m$)

34. _____ What is the boiling-point elevation of water for a solution that contains 125 g of barium nitrate, $Ba(NO_3)_2$, dissolved in 1.00 kg of water? The molar mass of the solute is 261.35 g/mol. ($K_b = 0.51°C/m$)

CHAPTER 15 TEST
Acids and Bases

MULTIPLE CHOICE On the line at the left of each statement, write the letter of the choice that best completes the statement or answers the question.

1. _____ The acid also known as muriatic acid is _____.

    a. nitric acid   **c.** hydrochloric acid

    b. sulfuric acid   **d.** phosphoric acid

2. _____ The acid manufactured in largest quantity is _____.

    a. hydrochloric acid   **c.** phosphoric acid

    b. nitric acid   **d.** sulfuric acid

3. _____ Which of the following is a strong base?

    a. NH_3 **c.** NaOH

    b. aniline   **d.** acetate ion

4. _____ In the reaction $HF(aq) + H_2O(l) \rightleftharpoons H_3O^+(aq) + F^-(aq)$, a conjugate acid-base pair is _____.

    a. F^- and H_2O **c.** HF and F^-

    b. H_3O^+ and HF   **d.** HF and H_2O

5. _____ If H_2O in the equation $H_2O + C_2H_3COOH \rightleftharpoons H_3O^+ + C_2H_3COO^-$ is a weak base, then H_3O^+ is a _____.

    a. stronger acid   **c.** weaker acid

    b. stronger base   **d.** weaker base

6. _____ Proton-transfer reactions favor production of the _____.

    a. stronger acid and stronger base

    b. weaker acid and weaker base

    c. stronger acid and weaker base

    d. weaker acid and stronger base

7. _____ Aqueous solutions of most bases contain _____.

    a. hydroxide ions and cations   **c.** hydrogen ions and anions

    b. hydroxide ions and anions   **d.** hydrogen ions and cations

8. _____ Acid strength increases with _____.

    a. increasing polarity and increasing bond strength

    b. increasing polarity and decreasing bond strength

    c. decreasing polarity and increasing bond strength

    d. decreasing polarity and decreasing bond strength

FILL IN THE BLANK   Write the correct term (or terms) in the space provided.

9. A substance that ionizes nearly completely in aqueous solutions, producing H_3O^+ ions, is a

_____ acid.

10. An acid that contains hydrogen and only one other element is called a(n)

_____ acid.

11. The species that remains after an acid has given up a proton is called the acid's

_____.

12. An acid that can donate two protons per molecule is called a(n)

_____ acid.

13. Bases are said to be neutralized when they react with _____ to

yield _____ and a(n) _____.

14. Any species that can react as either an acid or a base is described as

_____.

15. Barium carbonate will react with hydrochloric acid to produce _____,

_____, and _____.

Write the name of each of the following acids in the space provided.

16. _____ HNO_2

17. _____ HCl

18. _____ H_2CO_3

19. _____ H_2SO_4

20. _____ HI

21. _____ $HBrO$

Write the formula for each of the following acids in the space provided.

22. _____ hydrosulfuric acid

23. _____ nitric acid

24. _____ phosphorous acid

25. _____ perchloric acid

MODERN CHEMISTRY

Refer to the reaction below to answer questions 26 and 27.

$$HCl(g) + NH_3(l) \leftrightharpoons NH_4^+(aq) + Cl^-(aq)$$

26. List the conjugate acid-base pairs.

_____

_____

27. Identify each reactant and product as acidic or basic.

_____

_____

Refer to the reaction below to answer questions 28 and 29.

$$H_2O(l) + NH_3(g) \leftrightharpoons NH_4^+(aq) + OH^-(aq)$$

28. List the conjugate acid-base pairs.

_____

_____

29. Identify each reactant and product as a proton donor or a proton acceptor.

_____

_____

Refer to the following statement to answer questions 30–32:

Dilute HCl(aq) and NaOH(aq) are mixed in chemically equivalent quantities.

30. Write the formula equation for the reaction.

_____

31. Write the overall ionic equation for the reaction.

_____

32. Write the net ionic equation.

_____

CHAPTER 15 TEST continued

Use the following three acids to answer questions 33 and 34:

           iodic acid   **hypoiodous acid**   **periodic acid**

33. Give the formulas for these three acids.

_____   _____   _____

34. List the acids in order of increasing acid strength.

_____

SHORT ANSWER   Write the answers to the following questions in the space provided.

35. Explain the difference between strong acids and weak acids.

_____

_____

_____

36. Explain how the production of sulfur trioxide, SO_3, in industrial processes can result in acid rain. Write an equation for the reaction.

_____

_____

_____

_____

37. List five properties of aqueous acids.

_____

_____

_____

_____

38. Write the balanced equations that describe the three-stage ionization of phosphoric acid in a dilute aqueous solution.

_____

_____

_____

CHAPTER 16 TEST
Acid-Base Titration and pH

MULTIPLE CHOICE On the line at the left of each statement, write the letter of the choice that best completes the statement or answers the question.

1. _____ The pH scale in general use ranges from ____.

    a. 0 to 1   **c.** 0 to 7
    b. −1 to 1   **d.** 0 to 14

2. _____ During an acid-base titration, a very rapid change in pH occurs ____.

    a. when the first addition of known solution is made
    b. when roughly equivalent amounts of H_3O^+ and OH^- become present
    c. at several points
    d. at no point

3. _____ A water solution is neutral if ____.

    a. it contains no H_3O^+ ions
    b. it contains no ionized water molecules
    c. it contains no H_3O^+ or OH^- ions
    d. the concentrations of H_3O^+ and OH^- ions are equal

4. _____ The antilog of a number N is ____.

    a. the inverse of N
    b. the square root of N
    c. ten raised to the power of N
    d. raised to the tenth power

5. _____ Universal indicators ____.

    a. are mixtures of several indicator solutions
    b. are pure substances
    c. have very brief color-change intervals
    d. work well only for acidic solutions

6. _____ Which of the following is the pH range for an indicator that is useful in studying neutralizations involving strong acids and weak bases?

    a. 1.2 to 3.0   **c.** 6.0 to 7.6
    b. 3.1 to 4.6   **d.** 9.5 to 11.0

7. _____ An acid-base titration determines the solution volumes that are ____.

    a. chemically equivalent   **c.** of equal mass
    b. of equal molarity   **d.** of equal molality

8. _____ In acidic solutions, indicators are primarily in the form ____.

    a. In^+ **c.** $InOH$
    b. In^- **d.** HIn

FILL IN THE BLANK Write the correct term (or terms) in the space provided.

9. Pure water partially breaks down into charged particles in a process called

_____.

10. If $[H_3O^+]$ of a solution is less than $[OH^-]$, the solution is _____.

11. The pH range over which an indicator changes color is called the indicator's

_____.

12. The negative of the common logarithm of the hydronium-ion concentration is called

_____.

13. The product of $[H_3O^+]$ and $[OH^-]$ concentrations in water solution equals

_____.

14. The sum of the pH and the pOH of a neutral solution at 25°C is _____.

15. As the concentration of hydronium ions increases, a solution becomes more acidic and the pH

_____.

16. In a titration, an indicator changes color at the _____ of the titration.

17. When a weak acid is titrated with a strong base, the pH of the solution at the equivalence point is

_____ than 7.

18. When a strong acid is titrated with a weak base, the pH of the solution at the equivalence point is

_____ than 7.

19. A _____ is a highly purified solid used to check the concentration of a standard solution.

20. A 1 M solution of NaOH will have a pH that is _____ than the pH of a 1 M solution of NH_3.

In the space provided, identify each of the following values as true of *acidic* or *basic* solutions at 25°C.

21. _____ pH = 4.0

22. _____ $[H_3O^+] = 1 \times 10^{-2}$

23. _____ $[OH^-] = 1 \times 10^{-8}$

24. _____ pH = 9.0

25. _____ $[OH^-] = 1 \times 10^{-4}$

SHORT ANSWER Write the answers to the following questions in the space provided.

26. How does a pH meter measure the pH of a solution?

_____

_____

_____

27. What can be observed about the rate of change in the pH of a solution during a titration?

_____

_____

_____

_____

28. Write the general equilibrium expression for the dissociation of an acid-base indicator, and explain how this equilibrium determines the color of the indicator at a given pH.

_____

_____

_____

In the space provided, identify each of the following substances as *acidic*, *basic*, or *neutral*.

29. _____ grapefruit

30. _____ pure water

31. _____ sea water

32. _____ eggs

33. _____ blood

Calculate the $[H_3O^+]$ and $[OH^-]$ for each of the following. Write your answers in the spaces provided.

34. _____ 1×10^{-4} M HCl

35. _____ 1.0×10^{-4} M NaOH

36. _____ 1.0×10^{-4} M $Ca(OH)_2$

37. _____ 1×10^{-4} M HNO_3

38. _____ 5×10^{-3} M $HClO_4$

PROBLEMS Write the answers to the following problems on the line to the left, and show your work in the space provided.

39. _____ What is the hydronium ion concentration of an aqueous solution that has a pH of 5.0?

40. _____ What is the pH of a 10^{-4} M HCl solution?

41. _____ What is the hydroxide ion concentration of a solution with a pH of 12.40?

42. _____ What is the molarity of an H_2SO_4 solution if 49.0 mL of the solution is neutralized by 68.4 mL of an NaOH solution whose concentration is 0.333 M?

43. _____ If 72.1 mL of 0.543 M H_2SO_4 is needed to neutralize 39.0 mL of KOH solution, what is the molarity of the KOH solution?

44. _____ What is the molarity of an NaOH solution if 130.0 mL of the solution is neutralized by 61.3 mL of 0.0124 M H_3PO_4?

CHAPTER 17 TEST

Reaction Energy and Reaction Kinetics

MULTIPLE CHOICE   On the line at the left of each statement, write the letter of the choice that best completes the statement or answers the question.

1. _____ As compared with separate gases, a mixture of gases is _____.

    a. more disordered   **c.** equally disordered

    b. less disordered   **d.** less favorable

2. _____ A compound that is very unstable and likely to decompose violently would have a _____ heat of formation.

    a. small negative   **c.** large negative

    b. small positive   **d.** large positive

3. _____ In an energy-profile graph, the activated complex is represented at the _____.

    a. left end of the curve   **c.** bottom of the curve

    b. right end of the curve   **d.** top of the curve

4. _____ A rate law relates _____.

    a. reaction rate and temperature

    b. reaction rate and concentration

    c. temperature and concentration

    d. energy and concentration

5. _____ A reaction for which $\Delta H = -500$ kJ is _____.

    a. definitely spontaneous

    b. probably spontaneous

    c. probably nonspontaneous

    d. definitely nonspontaneous

6. _____ Examination of a chemical system before and after reaction reveals the _____.

    a. net chemical change   **c.** intermediates

    b. reaction mechanism   **d.** activated complex

7. _____ Increasing the surface area of reactants _____.

    a. tends to increase reaction rate

    b. tends to decrease reaction rate

    c. has no effect on reaction rate

    d. cancels the rate-determining step

8. _____ Which of the following is NOT directly measurable?

    a. heat of formation   **c.** enthalpy

    b. heat of combustion   **d.** change in enthalpy

FILL IN THE BLANK Write the correct term (or terms) in the space provided.

9. The sequence of steps in a reaction process is called the _____.

10. The study of the transfers of energy as heat that accompany chemical reactions and physical

changes is called _____.

11. Raising the _____ of a reaction increases the collision energy.

12. Free energy change depends on temperature, entropy change, and

_____ change.

13. The measure of the average kinetic energy of the particles in a sample of matter is its

_____.

14. Heat is measured in units called _____.

15. The energy transferred between samples of matter because of a difference in their temperatures

is called _____.

16. The energy absorbed or released as heat when 1 mol of a compound is formed from its elements is

the compound's _____.

17. A substance that increases the rate of a chemical reaction without being consumed is a(n)

_____.

18. The rate law for a reaction occurring by the one-step mechanism, $A + 2B \rightarrow AB_2$, is

_____; if the concentration of B is doubled, the rate is

_____.

MATCHING In the space to the left of each expression in the first column, write the letter of the expression in the second column that is most closely related.

19. _____ exothermic reaction   **a.** positive ΔG

20. _____ spontaneous reaction   **b.** positive ΔS

21. _____ reaction that increases disorder   **c.** positive ΔH

22. _____ reaction that decreases disorder   **d.** negative ΔG

23. _____ endothermic reaction   **e.** negative ΔS

     f. negative ΔH

CHAPTER 17 TEST continued

SHORT ANSWER Write the answers to the following questions in the space provided.

24. What is the difference between homogeneous reactions and heterogeneous reactions?

_____

_____

_____

_____

25. How does the energy of the activated complex compare with the energies of reactants and products?

_____

_____

_____

_____

26. List the five factors that influence reaction rate.

_____

_____

_____

_____

27. Explain the relationship between entropy change and the tendency for a reaction to occur.

_____

_____

_____

_____

28. Compare the enthalpy of products and reactants with the enthalpy change of endothermic and exothermic reactions.

_____

_____

_____

_____

CHAPTER 17 TEST continued

PROBLEMS Write the answers to the following problems on the line to the left, and show your work in the space provided.

29. _____ What is the value of ΔG at 120.0 K for a reaction in which $\Delta H = +35$ kJ/mol and $\Delta S = -1.50$ kJ/mol·K?

30. _____ Calculate the ΔG for the reaction $NaI(s) + Cl_2(g) \rightarrow NaCl(s) + I_2(l)$, given that $\Delta S = -79.9$ J/mol·K, $\Delta H_f^0(NaCl) = -385.9$ kJ/mol, and $\Delta H_f^0(NaI) = -287.9$ kJ/mol at 298 K.

31. _____ Determine the specific heat of a 70. g sample of material that absorbed 96 J as it was heated from 293 K to 313 K.

32. _____ What is the heat of combustion of a compound if its heat of formation is -520 kJ/mol and if the total heat of formation of its products is -670 kJ/mol (adjusted for the coefficients)?

33. _____ Use the equations below to calculate the heat of formation for propane gas, C_3H_8, from its elements, hydrogen gas and solid carbon.

$C_3H_8(g) + 5O_2(g) \rightarrow 3CO_2(g) + 4H_2O(l)$	$\Delta H_c^0 = -2219.2$ kJ/mol
$C(s) + O_2(g) \rightarrow CO_2(g)$	$\Delta H_c^0 = -393.5$ kJ/mol
$H_2(g) + \frac{1}{2}O_2(g) \rightarrow H_2O(l)$	$\Delta H_c^0 = -285.8$ kJ/mol

34. _____ For the vaporization reaction $Br_2(l) \rightarrow Br_2(g)$, $\Delta H^0 = 31.0$ kJ/mol and $\Delta S^0 = 93.0$ J/mol·K. At what temperature is this process spontaneous?

CHAPTER 18 TEST
Chemical Equilibrium

MULTIPLE CHOICE On the line at the left of each statement, write the letter of the choice that best completes the statement or answers the question.

1. _____ What is the effect on concentration if more $CO(g)$ is added to the following equilibrium system?

$$2CO(g) + O_2(g) \rightleftarrows 2CO_2(g)$$

    a. $[CO_2]$ increases and $[O_2]$ decreases
    b. $[CO_2]$ increases and $[O_2]$ increases
    c. $[CO_2]$ decreases and $[O_2]$ decreases
    d. both $[CO_2]$ and $[O_2]$ remain the same

2. _____ The equilibrium constant, K, for the ionization of acetic acid by the reaction
$CH_3COOH(aq) + H_2O(l) \rightleftarrows H_3O^+(aq) + CH_3COO^-(aq)$ is _____.

    a. $[H_3O^+][CH_3COO^-]$

    c. $\dfrac{[H_3O^+][CH_3COO^-]}{[CH_3COOH][H_2O]}$

    b. $\dfrac{[H_3O^+][CH_3COO^-]}{[CH_3COOH]}$

    d. $\dfrac{[CH_3COOH]}{[H_3O^+][CH_3COO^-]}$

3. _____ Adding the salt of a weak acid to a solution of the weak acid _____.

    a. lowers the concentration of the nonionized acid and of H_3O^+
    b. lowers the concentration of the nonionized acid and raises the concentration of H_3O^+
    c. raises the concentration of the nonionized acid and of H_3O^+
    d. raises the concentration of the nonionized acid and lowers the concentration of H_3O^+

4. _____ A very high value for K indicates that _____.

    a. reactants are favored
    b. products are favored
    c. equilibrium is reached slowly
    d. equilibrium has been reached

5. _____ How do K_a values for weak and strong acids compare?

    a. $K_a(weak) = K_a(strong)$
    b. $K_a(weak) < K_a(strong)$
    c. $K_a(weak) > K_a(strong)$
    d. K_a is not defined for weak acids

6. _____ A reaction in which products can reform reactants is said to be _____.

    a. at equilibrium
    b. reversible
    c. buffered
    d. impossible

7. _____ If the ion product for two ions whose solutions have just been mixed is greater than the value of K_{sp}, _____.

    a. precipitation occurs
    b. decomposition occurs
    c. the solution is unsaturated
    d. equilibrium cannot be achieved

FILL IN THE BLANK   Write the correct term (or terms) in the space provided.

8. Salts of a weak acid and a strong base produce solutions that are

_____.

9. The equation for the self-ionization of water is _____.

10. Hydrolysis is a reaction between water and _____.

11. Equilibrium is a _____ state.

12. The equilibrium expression for the reaction $PbNO_3(s) \rightleftarrows Pb^+(aq) + NO_3^-(aq)$ is

_____.

13. The phenomenon in which the addition of a charged particle common to two solutes decreases

solute concentration is called _____.

14. When small amounts of acids or bases are added to a solution of a weak acid and its salt, pH

_____.

15. At equilibrium, the rate of the forward reaction is _____ the rate
of the reverse reaction.

16. In a chemical equilibrium expression, the _____ shows
concentration of reactants.

17. The equilibrium constant equation for the reaction $NH_3 + H_2O \rightleftarrows NH_4^+ + OH^-$ is

_____.

18. If the temperature of an equilibrium system is decreased, the

_____ reaction will be favored.

19. A change in pressure affects only equilibrium systems containing reactants in the

_____.

20. If anions react with water, the process is called _____ and the
result is a more basic solution.

21. A solution that can resist changes in pH is called a(n) _____
solution.

22. The equilibrium expression for the ionization of the weak acid HA is

_____.

SHORT ANSWER Write the answers to the following questions in the space provided.

23. Name three ways that chemical equilibrium can be disturbed.

_____

_____

_____

24. Describe three situations in which ionic reactions go to completion.

_____

_____

_____

_____

In the space provided, predict the effect that decreasing pressure would have on each of the following reaction systems at equilibrium.

25. $H_2(g) + Cl_2(g) \rightleftarrows 2HCl(g)$ _____

26. $3O_2(g) \rightleftarrows 2O_3(g)$ _____

27. $CaCO_3(s) \rightleftarrows CaO(s) + CO_2(g)$ _____

In the space provided, identify the following salt solutions as *acidic*, *basic*, or *neutral*.

28. 0.5 M NaCl _____

29. 0.1 M NH_4NO_3 _____

30. 0.25 M $Ca(CH_3COO)_2$ _____

31. 0.50 M NH_4CH_3COO _____

32. 0.10 M NH_4Cl _____

In the space provided, state whether each system would produce an effective buffer solution.

33. H_3PO_4 and Na_3PO_4 _____

34. HCl and NaCl _____

35. KOH and KCH_3COO _____

36. NH_3 and NH_4Cl _____

PROBLEMS Write the answers to the following problems on the line to the left, and show your work in the space provided.

37. _____ At equilibrium a 1.0 L vessel contains 20.0 mol of H_2, 18.0 mol of CO_2, 12.0 mol of H_2O, and 5.9 mol of CO at 427°C. Calculate K at this temperature for the reaction $CO_2(g) + H_2(g) \rightleftarrows CO(g) + H_2O(g)$.

38. _____ Use the reaction $E + F \rightleftarrows 2G$ and the equilibrium concentrations 0.60 mol/L for E, 0.80 mol/L for F, and 1.30 mol/L for G to calculate the equilibrium constant.

39. _____ What is the concentration of H_3O^+ in a solution of an acid HY that ionizes to produce H_3O^+ and Y^- ions? K_a is 4.32×10^{-5}, and the final concentration of HY is 7.40×10^{-2} mol/L.

40. _____ Calculate the solubility product constant of barium carbonate, $BaCO_3$. The solubility of this compound is 0.0022 g/100. mL of water. (The atomic masses are C, 12.01; O, 16.00; Ba, 137.33.)

41. _____ What is the solubility in mol/L of copper(I) sulfide, Cu_2S? Its K_{sp} value is 6.1×10^{-49}.

42. _____ Calculate the ion product for 100 mL of 0.000 28 M $Pb(NO_3)_2$ mixed with 200 mL of 0.0012 M NaCl. K_{sp} for $PbCl_2$ is 1.9×10^{-4}. Does precipitation occur?

CHAPTER 19 TEST

Oxidation-Reduction Reactions

MULTIPLE CHOICE On the line at the left of each statement, write the letter of the choice that best completes the statement or answers the question.

1. _____ In the reaction $2K + Br_2 \rightarrow 2K^+ + 2Br^-$, which species is reduced?

    a. K only   **c.** both K and Br_2

    b. Br_2 only   **d.** neither K nor Br_2

2. _____ Which of the following is an example of autooxidation?

    a. $2H_2O_2 \rightarrow 2H_2O + O_2$

    b. $2H_2O \rightarrow H_3O^+ + OH^-$

    c. $Cu + 2AgNO_3 \rightarrow Cu(NO_3)_2 + 2Ag$

    d. $2Li + 2H_2O \rightarrow 2LiOH + H_2$

3. _____ In a cell used to electroplate silver onto an object, silver is _____ where it is deposited on the object to be plated.

    a. oxidized at the anode   **c.** oxidized at the cathode

    b. reduced at the anode   **d.** reduced at the cathode

4. _____ When a rechargeable cell is being recharged, the cell acts as a(n) _____.

    a. electrochemical cell   **c.** voltaic cell

    b. electrolytic cell   **d.** half-cell

5. _____ The half-reactions in the standard automobile battery use _____.

    a. lead(IV) oxide, lead, and sulfuric acid

    b. copper(II) oxide, copper, and sulfuric acid

    c. zinc oxide, zinc, and sulfuric acid

    d. iron(III) oxide, iron, and sulfuric acid

6. _____ In the reaction $Zn + CuSO_4 \rightarrow Cu + ZnSO_4$, _____.

    a. Cu is oxidized and Zn^{2+} is reduced

    b. Cu is reduced and Zn^{2+} is oxidized

    c. Cu^{2+} is oxidized and Zn is reduced

    d. Cu^{2+} is reduced and Zn is oxidized

7. _____ During redox reactions, reducing agents _____.

    a. attain a more negative oxidation state

    b. attain a more positive oxidation state

    c. keep the same oxidation state

    d. are not present

8. _____ If the calculated value for E^0_{cell} is negative, the reaction _____.

    a. occurs naturally in the direction written

    b. will not occur in a voltaic cell

    c. can be made to occur in a voltaic cell

    d. will occur naturally in an electrolytic cell

FILL IN THE BLANK   Write the correct term (or terms) in the space provided.

9. The electrode at which reduction occurs is the _____.

10. An oxidizing agent is a substance that is _____.

11. The oxidation number of oxygen in hydrogen peroxide is _____.

12. The branch of chemistry that deals with all electricity-related applications of oxidation-reduction reactions is called _____.

13. If reactants in a spontaneous energy-releasing oxidation-reduction reaction are connected externally by a wire conductor, energy is released as _____.

14. The oxidation number of nitrogen in NO_2 is _____.

15. When hydrogen peroxide decomposes naturally, the products are

_____ and _____.

16. In a voltaic cell, the half-reaction with the lower standard reduction potential takes place at the

_____.

17. A process in which a substance acts as both an oxidizing agent and a reducing agent is called

_____.

18. If the redox reaction in an electrochemical cell occurs naturally and produces electrical energy, the cell is a(n) _____.

19. In a zinc-carbon dry cell, the zinc container serves as the _____.

20. The difference in potential between an electrode and its solution is the

_____.

21. A process in which metal is deposited onto a surface by a nonspontaneous redox reaction is

_____.

22. The standard reference electrode for measuring electrode potentials is called a(n)

_____.

23. During oxidation-reduction reactions, the oxidation numbers of oxidizing agents

_____.

CHAPTER 19 TEST continued

In the space provided, label each of the following half-reactions as an *oxidation* half-reaction or a *reduction* half-reaction.

24. _____ $Br_2 + 2e^- \rightarrow 2Br^-$

25. _____ $Fe^{2+} + 2e^- \rightarrow Fe$

26. _____ $Fe^{2+} \rightarrow Fe^{3+} + e^-$

In the space provided, write the oxidation numbers for each atom in the following compounds.

27. _____ $CaCO_3$

28. _____ $Fe(NO_3)_2$

In the space provided, identify each of the following equations as *redox* or *nonredox* reactions.

29. _____ $2KNO_3(s) \rightarrow 2KNO_2(s) + O_2(g)$

30. _____ $SO_2(g) + H_2O(l) \rightarrow H_2SO_3(aq)$

31. _____ $H_2(g) + CuO(s) \rightarrow Cu(s) + H_2O(l)$

Use the table below to predict whether each of the following reactions will occur spontaneously as written by determining the E^0 value for the potential reaction.

Half-Reaction	E^0	Half-Reaction	E^0
$Cl_2 + 2e^- \rightleftarrows 2Cl^-$	+1.36 V	$Al^{3+} + 3e^- \rightleftarrows Al$	−1.66 V
$Cu^{2+} + 2e^- \rightleftarrows Cu$	+0.34 V	$Mg^{2+} + 2e^- \rightleftarrows Mg$	−2.37 V
$Sn^{2+} + 2e^- \rightleftarrows Sn$	−0.14 V	$K^+ + e^- \rightleftarrows K$	−2.93 V
$Zn^{2+} + 2e^- \rightleftarrows Zn$	−0.76 V	$Li^+ + e^- \rightleftarrows Li$	−3.04 V

32. _____ $Mg + Sn^{2+}$

34. _____ $Li^+ + Zn$

33. _____ $K + Al^{3+}$

35. _____ $Cu + Cl_2$

Use the figure of a voltaic cell below to answer questions 36–39. Recall that zinc is a more active reducing agent than copper.

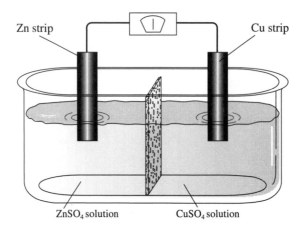

36. Which electrode is the anode? _____.

37. Write the half-reaction that takes place at the cathode.

_____

38. The electrons will flow from the _____ electrode to the

_____ electrode.

39. Sulfate ions in solution will move away from the _____

electrode and toward the _____ electrode.

In the space provided, write a balanced equation for the following redox reaction.

40. $K_2Cr_2O_7 + HCl \rightarrow KCl + CrCl_3 + H_2O + Cl_2$

Name _____ Date _____ Class _____

MULTIPLE CHOICE On the line at the left of each statement, write the letter of the choice that best completes the statement or answers the question.

1. _____ When a carbon atom forms four covalent bonds, the bonds are directed toward the corners of a ____.

    a. planar triangle   **c.** square

    b. pyramid   **d.** tetrahedron

2. _____ Which of the following carbon compounds is NOT an organic compound?

    a. aspirin   **c.** citric acid

    b. carbon dioxide   **d.** methane

3. _____ Which isomers can have different physical or chemical properties?

    a. structural isomers only

    b. geometric isomers only

    c. both structural isomers and geometric isomers

    d. neither structural isomers nor geometric isomers

4. _____ The general molecular formula for alkanes is ____.

    a. C_nH_{2n-2} **c.** C_nH_n

    b. C_nH_{2n} **d.** C_nH_{2n+2}

5. _____ Which of the following groups of compounds is saturated?

    a. alkenes   **c.** alkynes

    b. alkanes   **d.** aromatic hydrocarbons

6. _____ Which of the following is the structural formula for 2-methylpropane?

    a. $CH_3CH_2CH_3$ **c.** $CH_3CH_2CH_2CH_3$

    b. CH_3CHCH_3 **d.** $CH_3CHCH_2CH_3$

                CH_3 CH_3

7. _____ The hybridization on a carbon atom in an alkane is ____.

    a. sp^2 **c.** sp

    b. sp^4 **d.** sp^3

8. _____ Graphite is bonded in ____.

    a. layers of hexagonal plates

    b. squares

    c. a tetrahedral network

    d. an amorphous fashion

FILL IN THE BLANK   Write the correct term (or terms) in the space provided.

9. The colorless, crystalline solid form of carbon is _____.

10. _____ are electrons shared by more than two atoms.

11. The covalent bonding of an element to itself to form chains or rings is known as

   _____.

12. Hydrocarbons in which each carbon atom in the molecule forms four single covalent bonds with

   other atoms are called _____ hydrocarbons.

13. Alkanes with _____ or more carbon atoms have structural
   isomers.

14. The boiling point of alkanes _____ with increasing molecular
   mass.

15. A measure of a fuel's burning efficiency and anti-knock properties is its

   _____.

16. A simple straight-chain alkane with seven carbon atoms is called

   _____.

17. Diamond is a good conductor of _____.

18. Compounds that have the same molecular formula but different structures are called

   _____.

19. Organic compounds composed only of carbon and hydrogen are called

   _____.

20. Carbon atoms that form triple bonds have two _____ hybrid
   orbitals.

21. The general formula for noncyclic alkenes with one double bond is

   _____.

22. Complete combustion of hydrocarbons produces _____,

   _____, and _____.

23. A geometric isomer with functional groups on opposite sides of the molecule is called a(n)

   _____ isomer.

CHAPTER 20 TEST continued

SHORT ANSWER   Write the answers to the following questions in the space provided.

24. What properties of graphite fiber make it useful in sporting equipment and aircraft?

_____

_____

_____

25. Describe the structure of fullerenes.

_____

_____

_____

26. How do structural formulas differ from molecular formulas?

_____

_____

_____

27. Why are there no geometric isomers in noncyclic compounds containing single bonds?

_____

_____

_____

28. How does the trend in alkane boiling points apply to the fractional distillation of petroleum?

_____

_____

_____

Draw the condensed structural formula for each of the following compounds.

29. propane

31. 1,2-diethylbenzene

30. cyclopropane

32. 1-pentyne

MODERN CHEMISTRY

CHAPTER 20 TEST   **79**

HRW material copyrighted under notice appearing earlier in this work.

CHAPTER 20 TEST continued

Give the names of the following compounds.

33.

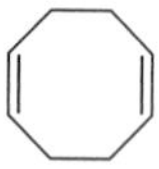

_____

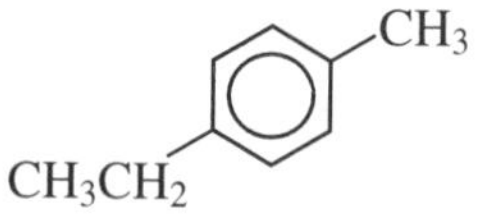

34.

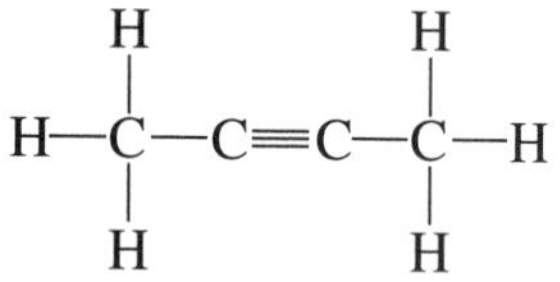

_____

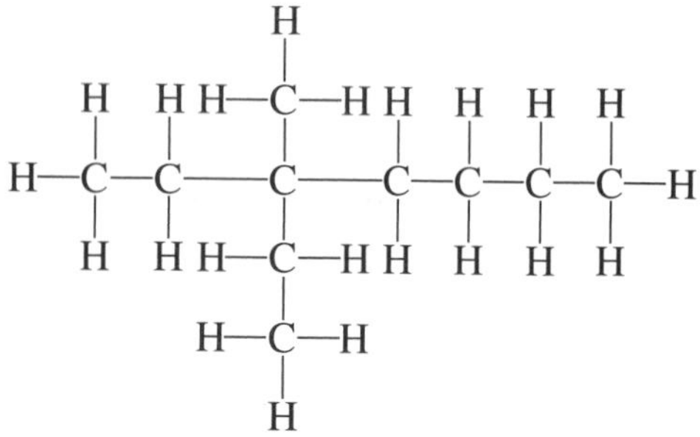

35.

_____

36. CH_3CH_2

_____

37.

_____

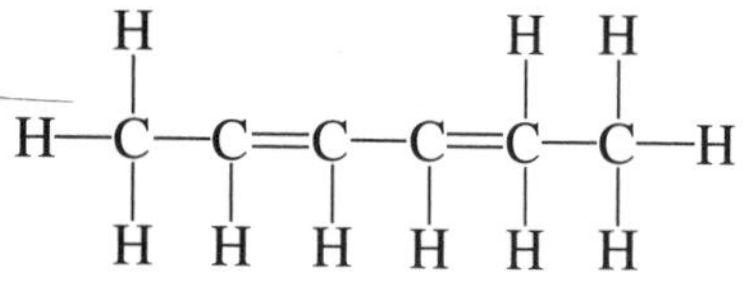

38.

_____

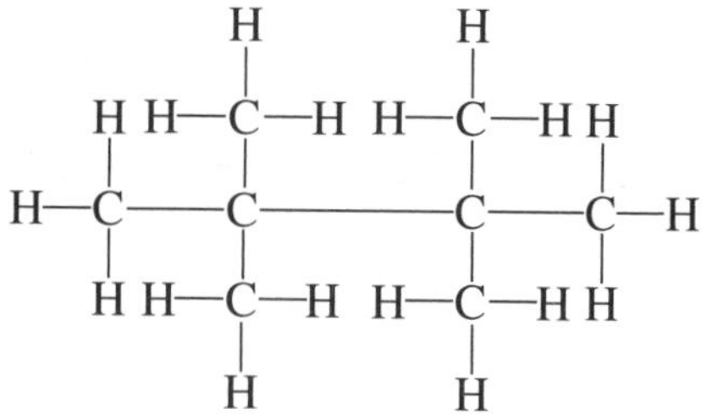

Label the following pairs as *structural isomers* or *geometric isomers*.

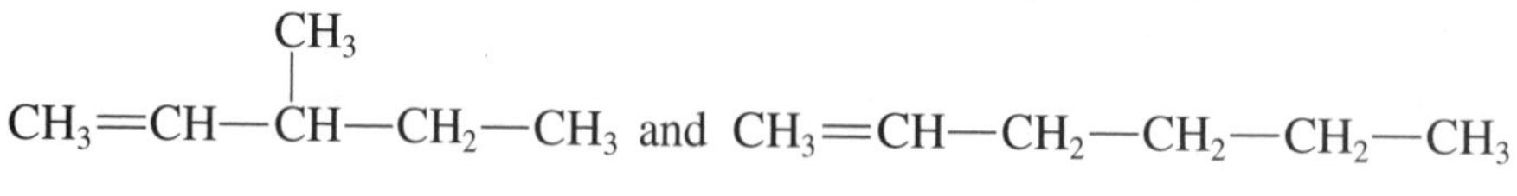

$CH_3{=}CH{-}\underset{\underset{CH_3}{|}}{CH}{-}CH_2{-}CH_3$ and $CH_3{=}CH{-}CH_2{-}CH_2{-}CH_2{-}CH_3$

39. _____

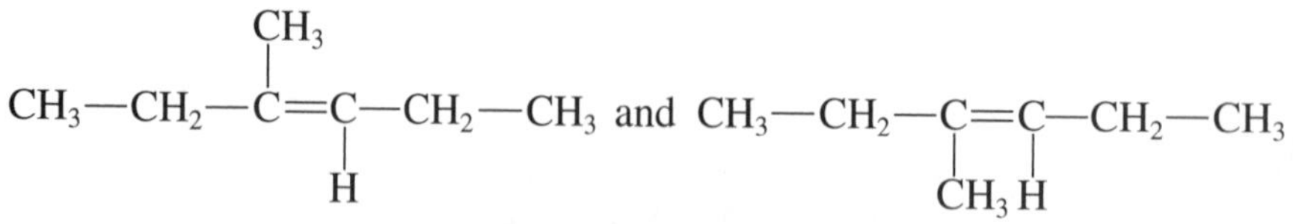

$CH_3{-}CH_2{-}\underset{\underset{H}{|}}{\overset{\overset{CH_3}{|}}{C}}{=}C{-}CH_2{-}CH_3$ and $CH_3{-}CH_2{-}C{=}\underset{\underset{H}{|}}{\overset{\overset{CH_3}{|}}{C}}{-}CH_2{-}CH_3$

40. _____

CHAPTER 21 TEST
Other Organic Compounds

MULTIPLE CHOICE On the line at the left of each statement, write the letter of the choice that best completes the statement or answers the question.

1. _____ A polymer that does not melt when heated but keeps its original shape is a ____ polymer.

    a. thermoplastic   **c.** linear

    b. thermosetting   **d.** branched

2. _____ Which of the following is used in making cold creams, lipsticks, and body lotions?

    a. ethanol   **c.** glycerol

    b. ethylene glycol   **d.** methanol

3. _____ Which of the following is used to give skis and cookware a nonsticking surface?

    a. dichlorodifluoromethane   **c.** tetrachloromethane

    b. tetrafluoroethene   **d.** polyvinylchloride

4. _____ Esters are frequently used ____.

    a. as water purifiers   **c.** in perfumes and flavorings

    b. as indicators   **d.** as electrolytes

5. _____ Compared with its corresponding unsaturated fatty acid, a saturated fatty acid has ____.

    a. more hydrogen   **c.** more oxygen

    b. less hydrogen   **d.** less oxygen

6. _____ Large molecules made of many small units joined to each other in organic reactions are

    _____.

    a. monomers   **c.** functional groups

    b. polymers   **d.** carboxylic acids

FILL IN THE BLANK Write the correct term (or terms) in the space provided.

7. The process in which adjacent polyisoprene molecules cross-link when they are heated with sulfur

    atoms is called _____.

8. An atom or group of atoms responsible for the properties of an organic compound is a(n)

    _____.

9. The hydrogenation of vegetable oil is an example of a(n) _____
    reaction.

10. The reaction between methane and chlorine in which a chlorine atom replaces a hydrogen atom in

    the methane molecule is an example of a(n) _____ reaction.

MATCHING   Match the general formula with its functional group.

11. _____ $R-\overset{\overset{\displaystyle O}{\|}}{C}-R'$

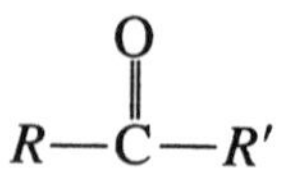

12. _____ $R-\overset{\overset{\displaystyle O}{\|}}{C}-O-R'$

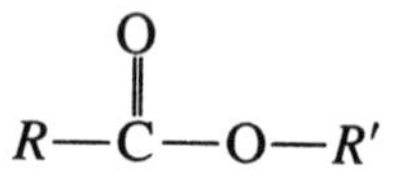

13. _____ $R-O-R'$

14. _____ $R-OH$

15. _____ $R-\underset{\underset{\displaystyle R'}{|}}{N}-R''$

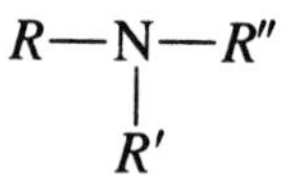

16. _____ $R-X$

17. _____ $R-\overset{\overset{\displaystyle O}{\|}}{C}-OH$

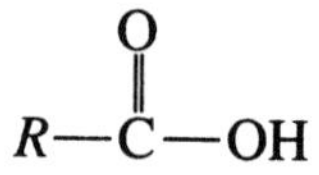

a. alcohol

b. alkyl halide

c. ether

d. aldehyde

e. ketone

f. carboxylic acid

g. ester

h. amine

In the space provided, write the name of the compound represented by the structural formulas shown.

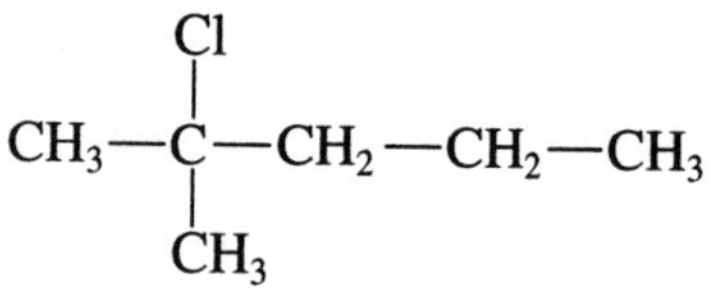

$CH_3-\underset{\underset{\displaystyle CH_3}{|}}{\overset{\overset{\displaystyle Cl}{|}}{C}}-CH_2-CH_2-CH_3$

18. _____

$CH_3-CH_2-O-CH_3$

19. _____

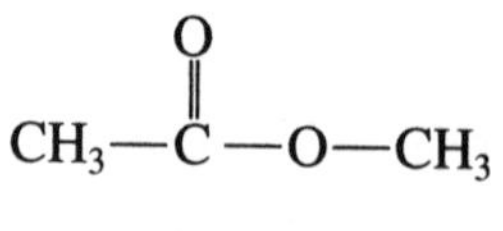

$CH_3-\overset{\overset{\displaystyle O}{\|}}{C}-O-CH_3$

20. _____

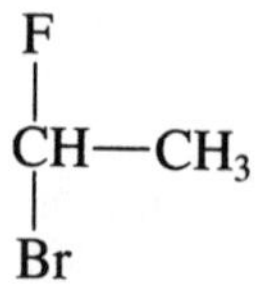

$\underset{\underset{\displaystyle Br}{|}}{\overset{\overset{\displaystyle F}{|}}{C}H}-CH_3$

21. _____

CHAPTER 21 TEST continued

$$CH_3-CH_2-O-CH_2-CH_3$$

22. _____

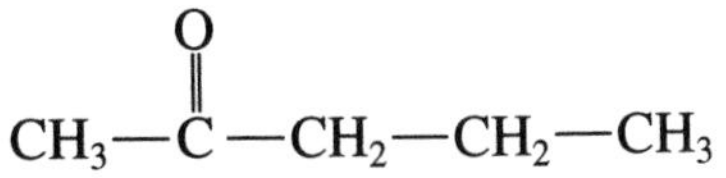

$$CH_3-\overset{\overset{\displaystyle O}{\|}}{C}-CH_2-CH_2-CH_3$$

23. _____

Draw the structural formula for each of the following compounds.

24. 2-butanol

25. 1,1,1,2-tetrabromobutane

26. butyl methyl ether

27. propanal

28. methanoic acid

29. tripropylamine

MODERN CHEMISTRY

Identify each of the following reactions as a *substitution, addition, condensation,* or *elimination.*

$$CH_3-OH + CH_3-\overset{\overset{\displaystyle O}{\|}}{C}-OH \rightarrow CH_3-\overset{\overset{\displaystyle O}{\|}}{C}-O-CH_3 + H_2O$$

30. _____

$$CH_3-CH_2-CH_2-CH_3 + Cl_2 \rightarrow Cl-CH_2-CH_2-CH_2-CH_3 + HCl$$

31. _____

$$CH_2{=}CH_2 + Cl_2 \rightarrow Cl-CH_2-CH_2-Cl$$

32. _____

SHORT ANSWER Write the answers to the following questions in the space provided.

33. Explain why the boiling points of alcohols are higher than the boiling points of alkanes with similar molecular masses.

_____

_____

_____

34. Explain how CFC-12 (dichlorodifluoromethane) can deplete the ozone layer.

_____

_____

_____

35. What is the difference between aldehydes and ketones?

_____

_____

_____

36. Can an addition reaction occur between propane and chlorine? Why or why not?

_____

_____

_____

CHAPTER 22 TEST

Nuclear Chemistry

MULTIPLE CHOICE On the line at the left of each statement, write the letter of the choice that best completes the statement or answers the question.

1. _____ After converting units, the nuclear mass defect is equivalent to the _____.

    a. atomic mass

    b. electrostatic force

    c. energy of chemical reaction

    d. nuclear binding energy

2. _____ For atoms of low atomic number, the most stable nuclei have a neutron-proton ratio _____.

    a. much less than 1:1

    b. approximately 1:1

    c. between 1:1 and 1.5:1

    d. greater than 1.5:1

3. _____ All nuclides beyond _____ in the periodic table are radioactive.

    a. lead

    b. bismuth

    c. mercury

    d. gold

4. _____ The elements with the greatest binding energies are the _____.

    a. most stable

    b. smallest in size

    c. least stable

    d. largest in size

5. _____ Most stable nuclei have _____.

    a. odd numbers of both protons and neutrons

    b. even numbers of both protons and neutrons

    c. odd numbers of protons and even numbers of neutrons

    d. even numbers of protons and odd numbers of neutrons

6. _____ In a nuclear reactor, control rods _____.

    a. cool the reactor

    b. slow neutrons

    c. protect against radioactivity

    d. absorb some free neutrons

7. _____ If a 100 g sample of an isotope with a half-life of 10 years decays for 20 years, _____ will remain.

    a. 50 g

    b. 10 g

    c. 25 g

    d. 0 g

FILL IN THE BLANK Write the correct term (or terms) in the space provided.

8. The time required for half the atoms in a sample of a radioactive nuclide to undergo decay is called

_____.

9. The sun and other stars produce energy by the process of _____.

10. A change in the identity of a nucleus due to a change in the number of its protons is called a(n)

_____.

11. The spontaneous disintegration of a nucleus into a slightly less massive and more stable nucleus with emission of particles and/or electromagnetic radiation is

_____.

12. _____ are elements with more than 92 protons in their nuclei.

13. High-energy electromagnetic waves emitted from a nucleus as it changes from an excited state to a ground energy state are _____.

14. The amount of radiation that produces 2×10^9 ion pairs when it passes through 1 cm^3 of dry air is a(n) _____.

15. Radiation damage to human tissue is measured in _____.

MATCHING On the line at the left of each term in the first column, write the letter of the symbol in the second column that is most closely related.

16. _____ alpha particle   **a.** $_{+1}^{0}\beta$

17. _____ beta particle   **b.** γ

18. _____ gamma ray   **c.** $_{2}^{4}\text{He}$

19. _____ positron   **d.** $_{-1}^{0}\beta$

In the space provided, identify each of the following nuclear reactions as an *alpha decay, beta decay, positron emission,* or *electron capture.*

20. _____ $_{6}^{14}\text{C} \rightarrow _{7}^{14}\text{N} + _{-1}^{0}\beta$

21. _____ $_{47}^{106}\text{Ag} + _{-1}^{0}e \rightarrow _{46}^{106}\text{Pd}$

22. _____ $_{84}^{210}\text{Po} \rightarrow _{82}^{206}\text{Pb} + _{2}^{4}\text{He}$

23. _____ $_{19}^{38}\text{K} \rightarrow _{18}^{38}\text{Ar} + _{+1}^{0}\beta$

Complete each of the following equations.

24. $_{88}^{226}\text{Ra} \rightarrow _{86}^{222}\text{Rn} + $ _____

25. $_{4}^{9}\text{Be} + _{2}^{4}\text{He} \rightarrow _{6}^{12}\text{C} + $ _____

26. $_{90}^{234}\text{Th} \rightarrow _{91}^{234}\text{Pa} + $ _____

27. $_{75}^{187}\text{Re} + $ _____ $\rightarrow _{75}^{188}\text{Re} + _{1}^{1}\text{H}$

MODERN CHEMISTRY

CHAPTER 22 TEST continued

SHORT ANSWER   Write the answers to the following questions in the space provided.

28. Define artificial radioactive isotopes, and explain how they are produced.

_____

_____

_____

29. Compare the penetrating powers of alpha particles, beta particles, and gamma rays.

_____

_____

_____

30. Describe fission, and explain how it is used in a nuclear reactor.

_____

_____

_____

31. Describe fusion, and explain how it is used in a hydrogen bomb.

_____

_____

_____

32. What is a chain reaction?

_____

_____

_____

33. List the five main components of a nuclear reactor.

_____

_____

_____

PROBLEMS Write the answers to the following questions on the line to the left, and show your work in the space provided.

proton mass = 1.007 276 amu
neutron mass = 1.008 665 amu
electron mass = 0.000 5486 amu
speed of light = 2.997 925 × 10^8 m/s
1 amu = 1.6605 × 10^{-27} kg

34. _____ Calculate the nuclear binding energy of a $^{32}_{16}$S atom. The measured atomic mass of $^{32}_{16}$S is 31.972 070 amu.

35. _____ Calculate the mass defect of an $^{16}_{8}$O atom. The measured atomic mass of $^{16}_{8}$O is 15.994 915 amu.

36. _____ Calculate the nuclear binding energy per nucleon of a $^{89}_{35}$Br atom. The measured atomic mass of $^{89}_{35}$Br is 88.926 550 amu.

37. _____ The half-life of an isotope is 30. s. In a 1000. g sample, what mass of this isotope remains after 5.0 min?

38. _____ After how many days does 1/32 of a sample of radon-222 remain? The half-life of this isotope is 3.824 days.

CHAPTER TESTS ANSWER KEY

1 *Matter and Change,* pp. 1–4

1. c
2. d
3. a
4. d
5. c
6. c
7. c
8. a
9. mass and volume
10. group or family
11. homogeneous
12. products
13. metal
14. solid state
15. chemical properties
16. atom
17. compound
18. nonmetal
19. mixture
20. pure substance
21. basic
22. metalloid
23. reactants: carbon and oxygen; product: carbon dioxide
24. reactant: mercury(II) oxide; products: mercury and oxygen
25. f
26. g
27. c
28. a
29. b
30. i
31. d
32. h
33. e
34. physical change
35. chemical change
36. physical change
37. physical change
38. chemical change
39. physical change
40. In a solid, particles are packed together in relatively fixed positions. The particles vibrate about a fixed point. In a liquid, particles are close together but can flow around one another. In a gas, particles are at great distances from one another, compared to the particles of liquids and solids.
41. The composition of a pure substance is the same throughout and does not vary from sample to sample. Pure substances include elements and compounds. A mixture contains more than one substance and can vary in composition from one sample to another and sometimes within different parts of the same sample.
42. Although energy can be absorbed or released in a change, it is not destroyed or created. It simply takes a different form.
43. Homogeneous mixtures are uniform in composition; heterogeneous mixtures are not.
44. An element cannot be broken down, but water can be decomposed into hydrogen and oxygen by passing an electrical current through it (electrolysis).

2 *Measurements and Calculations,* pp. 5–8

1. a
2. c
3. c
4. a
5. c
6. c
7. a
8. a
9. time
10. mass
11. density
12. energy
13. length or distance
14. volume
15. area
16. qualitative
17. quantitative
18. qualitative
19. quantitative
20. 3.00×10^5 km/s
21. three
22. 0.026 g or 2.6×10^{-2} g
23. 2.5×10^{-1} L
24. quantity
25. derived units
26. conversion factor
27. 0.0432 kg or 4.32×10^{-2} kg
28. 5400 mL or 5.4×10^3 mL
29. 300. K
30. 1.05×10^3 J
31. 3.51×10^3 cm
32. A hypothesis is a testable statement that can be used to make predictions and to carry out further experiments. A theory is a broad generalization that explains a body of facts or phenomena.
33. Mass is a measure of the quantity of matter. Weight is a measure of the gravitational pull on matter. Mass does not depend on gravitational attraction.
34. Models are visual, verbal, or mathematical representations. They are used to explain how phenomena occur or how data or events are related.
35. The graph of two quantities that are directly proportional is a straight line through the origin.

The graph of two quantities that are inversely proportional is a curve called a hyperbola.

36. 2.20 g/cm^3
37. -3%
38. 114 g
39. $8.12 \times 10^{-2} \text{ L}$
40. 3.164 g

3 Atoms: The Building Blocks of Matter, *pp. 9–12*

1. c **5.** d
2. c **6.** c
3. c **7.** b
4. b **8.** c
9. definite proportions
10. mole
11. electrons
12. atom
13. isotopes
14. mass
15. nuclear forces
16. atomic
17. multiple proportions
18. mass
19. 1; 1+; in the nucleus
20. 1; 0; in the nucleus
21. 0; 1−; outside the nucleus (in the electron cloud)
22. Answers should include three of the following:
All matter is composed of extremely small particles called atoms.
All atoms of an element are identical in size, mass, and other properties; atoms of different elements differ in size, mass and other properties. Atoms cannot be subdivided, created, or destroyed.
Atoms of different elements combine in simple whole-number ratios to form chemical compounds.
In chemical reactions, atoms are combined, separated, or rearranged.
23. The molar mass of a substance is the mass of one mole of the substance. A mole of any substance contains 6.022137×10^{23} particles, or Avogadro's number of particles. The atomic mass is the mass of one atom.
24. The atomic mass of a single isotope of an element is its relative mass compared to the mass of carbon-12. The average atomic mass of an element is the weighted average of the masses of all naturally occurring isotopes of an element.
25. 32
26. 6
27. 14

28. 15.999 amu
29. 156 g
30. 5.300 mol
31. 1.205×10^{23} atoms
32. 1.204×10^{24} atoms

4 Arrangement of Electrons in Atoms, *pp. 13–16*

1. c **5.** c
2. d **6.** b
3. d **7.** a
4. b **8.** a
9. noble gas
10. frequency or wavelength
11. longer
12. hertz
13. wavelength
14. photoelectric effect
15. ground state
16. frequency
17. line-emission
18. $3.00 \times 10^8 \text{ m/s}$
19. red
20. Heisenburg uncertainty principle
21. inner-shell electrons
22. electromagnetic radiation
23. d
24. a
25. b
26. c
27. the photoelectric effect and the line-emission spectrum of hydrogen
28. A line-emission spectrum is produced when an electron drops from a higher-energy orbit to one with lower energy, emitting a photon whose energy is equal to the difference in energy between the two orbits.
29. $1s^2 2s^2 2p^5$
30. $1s^2 2s^2 2p^6 3s^2 3p^4$
31. $1s^2 2s^2 2p^6 3s^2 3p^6 4s^2$
32. $1s^2 2s^2 2p^6 3s^2 3p^6 3d^6 4s^2$
33. $[\text{He}] 2s^2 2p^2$
34. $[\text{He}] 2s^2 2p^6$
35. $[\text{Xe}] 6s^2$
36. $[\text{Ar}] 4s^1$

37. $\underset{1s}{\uparrow\downarrow}$ $\underset{2s}{\uparrow}$

38. $\underset{1s}{\uparrow\downarrow}$ $\underset{2s}{\uparrow\downarrow}$ $\underset{2p_x}{\uparrow}$ $\underset{2p_y}{\uparrow}$ $\underset{2p_z}{}$

39. $\underset{1s}{\uparrow\downarrow}$ $\underset{2s}{\uparrow\downarrow}$ $\underset{2p_x}{\uparrow\downarrow}$ $\underset{2p_y}{\uparrow\downarrow}$ $\underset{2p_z}{\uparrow\downarrow}$

40. 7.05×10^{16} Hz
41. 1.28 s
42. 4.58×10^{-19} J

5 The Periodic Law, pp. 17–20

1. a
2. c
3. d
4. d
5. a
6. a
7. d
8. a
9. lanthanides
10. 2
11. fourth
12. transition elements
13. 32
14. valence electrons
15. electron affinity
16. electronegativity
17. ionization energy
18. $3s^23p^4$
19. atomic radius
20. ion
21. Group 1, seventh period, *s* block
22. All three are metals. Alkali and alkaline earth metals are so reactive that they do not occur alone in nature. Transition elements are much less reactive; some are nearly non-reactive.
23. All the elements are in the third period. Of the four, sodium has the lowest atomic number and is the first element in the period. Therefore, sodium has the largest atomic radius because atomic radii decrease across a period.
24. Ionization energies increase across a period and decrease down a group.
25. Both electron affinity and electronegativity measure an atom's ability to attract electrons. Electron affinity is the energy change when an atom gains an electron. Electronegativity measures the relative ability of atoms of different elements to attract electrons.
26. The physical and chemical properties of the elements are periodic functions of their atomic numbers.
27. Cations are always smaller than the atoms from which they are formed; anions are always larger than the atoms from which they are formed.
28. c
29. b
30. e
31. a
32. d
33. Period 5, *s* block
34. Period 4, *p* block
35. Period 4, *d* block

36. $3d^54s^2$
37. $3s^23p^3$
38. $4f^{14}5d^{10}6s^2$
39. 1+, helium
40. 2−, neon
41. 2−, argon
42. 3+, neon

6 Chemical Bonding, pp. 21–24

1. a
2. c
3. a
4. b
5. c
6. d
7. c
8. a
9. polar-covalent bond
10. diatomic molecule
11. electronegativities
12. molecule
13. H·
14. chemical formula
15. polyatomic ion
16. double bond
17. formula unit
18. bond energy
19. metallic bond
20. ductility
21. linear
22. tetrahedral
23. octahedral
24. :N ≡ N:
25. H—Cl:
26.

$$:\ddot{I}:$$
$$|$$
$$:\ddot{I}—C—\ddot{I}:$$
$$|$$
$$:\ddot{I}:$$

27.

$$\ddot{O}$$
$$H \quad H$$

28. Hydrogen bonding, a particularly strong dipole-dipole force, causes a powerful attraction between water molecules that results in a high boiling point.
29. One *s* orbital and three *p* orbitals combine to form four bonding orbitals of equal energy.
30. Ionic bonding involves the electrical attraction between large numbers of anions and cations. Covalent bonding involves the sharing of electron pairs between two atoms.
31. Most atoms are at lower potential energy when bonded to other atoms than they are as independent particles. Nature favors arrangements with low potential energy.

32. Compound A is probably ionic. The ionic attraction is stronger than the intermolecular attractions, resulting in higher melting and boiling points.

33. Metals are malleable and ductile because one plane of atoms can slide past another without encountering any resistance or breaking any bonds, while the shifting of layers in an ionic crystal breaks its bonds and shatters the crystal.

34. Some molecules and ions cannot be adequately represented by a single Lewis structure. The actual structure of these molecules lies somewhere between the resonance structures.

35. nonpolar covalent
36. ionic
37. ionic
38. polar covalent
39. ionic
40. polar covalent

7 Chemical Formulas and Chemical Compounds, *pp. 25–28*

1. c
2. d
3. d
4. b
5. d
6. d
7. c
8. b
9. +6
10. −1
11. +2
12. +4
13. SiO_2
14. CI_4
15. $Sn(CrO_4)_2$
16. $Ba(OH)_2$
17. phosphorus(III) iodide
18. dinitrogen tetroxide
19. iron(II) nitrite
20. carbon tetrachloride
21. carbon monoxide
22. copper(II) carbonate
23. $CaCl_2$, calcium chloride
24. $PbCrO_4$, lead(II) chromate
25. $Al_2(SO_4)_3$, aluminum sulfate
26. $Sn_3(PO_4)_4$, tin(IV) phosphate
27. cyanide ion
28. oxide ion
29. hydroxide ion
30. S^{2-}
31. Cu^+
32. CO_3^{2-}
33. H, +1; O, −1

34. C, +4; O, −2
35. N, −3; H, +1
36. 323.5 g/mol
37. 134.45 amu
38. 47.27% Cu, 52.73% Cl
39. 43.2 g
40. CF_4
41. C_4H_{10}
42. C_2H_6

8 Chemical Equations and Reactions, *pp. 29–32*

1. b
2. a
3. b
4. d
5. a
6. b
7. d
8. a
9. coefficient
10. liquid
11. reversible reaction
12. $A + X \rightarrow AX$
13. $AX \rightarrow A + X$
14. $A + BX \rightarrow AX + B$
15. $AX + BY \rightarrow AY + BX$
16. metal hydroxides
17. combustion reaction
18. electrolysis
19. activity series
20. chemical equation
21. conservation of mass
22. gaseous
23. heated
24. A word equation and a formula equation are both qualitative. Although they both show the reactants and products of a chemical reaction, they give no information about amounts of reactants or products. A chemical equation, however, does show the relative amounts of the reactants and products in a chemical reaction.
25. Three indications of a chemical reaction are the radiation of heat and light, the production of a gas, and the formation of a precipitate.
26. zinc sulfide + oxygen →
zinc oxide + sulfur dioxide
27. sodium iodide + chlorine →
sodium chloride + iodine
28. $Mg + O_2 \rightarrow MgO$
29. $CaCO_3 \rightarrow CaO + CO_2$
30. decomposition reaction
31. single-replacement reaction
32. synthesis reaction
33. double-replacement reaction
34. $2AgNO_3 + CuCl_2 \rightarrow 2AgCl + Cu(NO_3)_2$

35. $2PbO_2 \rightarrow 2PbO + O_2$

36. $Zn(OH)_2 + 2CH_3COOH \rightarrow$
$$Zn(CH_3COO)_2 + 2H_2O$$

37. $Mg(s) + 2H_2O(g) \rightarrow Mg(OH)_2(aq) + H_2(g)$

38. no reaction

39. $Cl_2(g) + MgBr_2(aq) \rightarrow MgCl_2(aq) + Br_2(l)$

40. $Zn(s) + 2HCl(aq) \rightarrow ZnCl_2(aq) + H_2(g)$

41. no reaction

42. $Ni(s) + CuCl_2(aq) \rightarrow NiCl_2(aq) + Cu(s)$

43. no reaction

44. $Mg(s) + Co(NO_3)_2(aq) \rightarrow Mg(NO_3)_2(aq) + Co(s)$

9 *Stoichiometry,* *pp. 33–36*

1. c
2. b
3. d
4. a
5. a
6. a
7. a
8. b

9. given: mass of NH_3 = 500 g
unknown: mass of N_2

10. given: mass of H_2O = 500 g
unknown: amount of H_2

11. given: amount of CO_2 = 20 mol
unknown: mass of CO

12. given: amount of H_2O = 50 mol
unknown: amount of O_2

13. given: mass of SO_2 = 800 g
unknown: mass of S

14. percent yield = $\dfrac{\text{actual yield}}{\text{theoretical yield}} \times 100$

15. moles of A $\rightarrow$ moles of B

16. $\dfrac{1 \text{ mol } C_7H_6O_3}{138.13 \text{ g } C_7H_6O_3}$

17. limiting reactant

18. actual yield

19. excess reactant

20. 70.0 g

21. 575 g FeO

22. 19.4 mol O_2

23. 0.904 mol PbI_2

24. 409 g $KClO_3$

25. 1.03×10^3 g CO_2

26. 4.48 g H_2

27. 83.88%

28. 1.00 mol KCl

29. 188 g KCl

30. 91.0%

10 *Physical Characteristics of Gases,* *pp. 37–40*

1. a
2. c
5. c
6. a

3. a
4. c
7. a

8. pressure

9. temperature

10. 760 mm

11. $V'P' = VP$

12. kinetic-molecular theory

13. effusion

14. ideal gas

15. diffusion

16. pressure

17. newton

18. barometer

19. partial pressure

20. decrease

21. absolute zero

22. elastic

23. fluids

24. c

25. d

26. a

27. e

28. b

29. 570 mm Hg

30. 40 atm

31. 150°C

32. 950. mL

33. 91°C

34. 12.5 atm

35. 459 mm Hg

36. 6.8 atm

37. 236 L

38. 426 mL

11 *Molecular Composition of Gases,* *pp. 41–44*

1. b
2. c
3. b
4. a
5. b
6. b
7. d

8. two

9. 22.4 L

10. effusion

11. Avogadro's law

12. *nRT*

13. Boyle's

14. 1:2

15. temperature

16. c

17. e

18. a

19. f

20. b
21. 24 L
22. 16.8 L
23. 16 g/mol
24. 2.05 g/L
25. 101 g
26. 0.77 L
27. 3.36 atm
28. 116 g/mol
29. 13.1 L
30. 22.3 g
31. 2 times
32. 137 g

12 *Liquids and Solids,* *pp. 45–48*

1. b   **5.** b
2. c   **6.** c
3. c   **7.** c
4. b   **8.** a
9. critical temperature
10. surface tension
11. amorphous
12. equilibrium vapor pressure
13. triple point
14. molar heat of fusion
15. unit cell
16. metallic
17. C
18. E
19. G
20. A
21. D
22. F
23. B
24. H
25. According to the kinetic-molecular theory, the particles in a liquid can change relative positions but still are influenced by attractive forces. Their ability to move about explains the fluidity of liquids and their ability to diffuse. As some particles at the surface of a liquid gain energy, they overcome the attractive force and vaporize.
26. In ionic crystals, monatomic or polyatomic positive and negative ions are arranged in a regular pattern. In metallic crystals, metal atoms are surrounded by a sea of valence electrons. The electrons are donated by the metal atoms and belong to the crystal as a whole.
27. At high elevations, water boils at a lower temperature. A liquid boils when its equilibrium vapor pressure is equal to atmospheric pressure. The lowered atmospheric pressure at high

elevations means the equilibrium vapor pressure will equal atmospheric pressure at a lower temperature.
28. Ionic crystals are hard and brittle, have high melting points, and are good insulators. Covalent network crystals are nearly always hard and brittle. They have rather high melting points and are usually nonconductors or semiconductors. Metallic crystals vary greatly in melting points and are good conductors. Covalent molecular crystals are easily vaporized, are relatively soft, and are good insulators.
29. Increasing the temperature of a liquid increases its average kinetic energy. That in turn increases the number of molecules that have enough energy to escape from the liquid phase into the vapor phase. This increased evaporation rate increases the concentration of molecules in the vapor phase, which increases the equilibrium vapor pressure.
30. d
31. f
32. h
33. g
34. c
35. b
36. i
37. a
38. 15.7 kJ
39. 9.95 kJ/mol
40. 1.48 kJ

13 *Solutions,* *pp. 49–52*

1. b   **5.** b
2. c   **6.** a
3. a   **7.** d
4. a   **8.** c
9. decreases
10. solute
11. colloid
12. equilibrium
13. nonpolar
14. ions
15. supersaturated solution
16. particle size
17. solution
18. exothermic
19. hydration
20. immiscible
21. solvated
22. hydrate
23. increase
24. alloy

25. "Like dissolves like" means that polar solvents dissolve polar solutes, and nonpolar solvents dissolve nonpolar solutes.

26. Both terms are ways of expressing the concentration of solutions. Molarity is the number of moles of solute per liter of solution. Molality is the number of moles of solute per kilogram of solvent.

27. Solutions are homogeneous mixtures. Suspensions and colloids are heterogeneous mixtures. Solutions have the smallest particle size, followed by the size of colloid particles and suspension particles. Solutions and colloids do not settle out on standing, but suspensions do. Solutions and colloids cannot be separated by filtration, but suspensions can be. Solutions do not scatter light. Colloids scatter light. Suspensions may scatter light, but they are not transparent.

28. Nonpolar substances are generally soluble in nonpolar liquids. Water molecules are polar. Since ethanol dissolves in water, its molecules must also be polar. Since carbon tetrachloride does not dissolve in water, its molecules must be nonpolar.

29. 10.0 g/100 g H_2O
30. 6.07 kg
31. 12.0 g
32. 8.2 g
33. 24.4 g
34. 0.0846 M
35. 1.67 L
36. 0.799 m $C_{12}H_{22}O_{11}$

14 Ions in Aqueous Solutions and Colligative Properties, pp. 53–56

1. a
2. d
3. d
4. d
5. b
6. b
7. d
8. a
9. precipitation
10. semi-permeable membrane
11. electrolyte
12. spectator ion
13. three
14. osmotic pressure
15. H_3O^+
16. $Ca(NO_3)_2$
17. greater
18. lower
19. $2K^+(aq) + S^{2-}(aq)$
20. Dissociation is the separation of ions that occurs when an ionic compound dissolves. The ions are already present separate from one another. Ionization is the process of forming ions from the solute molecules by the action of the solvent. When a molecular compound dissolves and ionizes in a polar solvent, ions are formed.

21. In a strong electrolyte, all or almost all of the dissolved compound exists as ions in aqueous solution. In a weak electrolyte, little of the dissolved compound exists as ions in aqueous solution.

22. When a compound containing hydrogen dissolves in water to form a hydrogen ion, H^+, the H^+ ion attracts other molecules or ions so strongly that it rarely exists alone. In water, the H^+ ion immediately bonds to a water molecule, forming a hydronium ion, H_3O^+.

23. Dissolved salt will lower the freezing point of water. Therefore, adding salt to icy roads will help melt the ice and prevent further freezing of any water on the road's surface. It will also prevent the refreezing of water as it melts.

24. none
25. $Ba^{2+}(aq) + SO_4^{2-}(aq) \rightarrow BaSO_4(s)$
26. $Cd^{2+}(aq) + S^{2-}(aq) \rightarrow CdS(s)$
27. none
28. none
29. 42 g/mol
30. 0.77°C/m
31. −0.261°C
32. −2.81°C/m
33. 690 g
34. 0.73°C

15 Acids and Bases, pp. 57–60

1. c
2. d
3. c
4. c
5. a
6. b
7. a
8. b
9. strong
10. binary
11. conjugate base
12. diprotic
13. acids, water, salt
14. amphoteric
15. carbon dioxide, barium chloride, water
16. nitrous acid
17. hydrochloric acid
18. carbonic acid
19. sulfuric acid
20. hydriodic acid
21. hypobromous acid
22. H_2S
23. HNO_3

24. H_3PO_3

25. $HClO_4$

26. HCl and Cl^-
NH_3 and NH_4^+

27. acidic: HCl and NH_4^+
basic: NH_3 and Cl^-

28. H_2O and OH^-
NH_3 and NH_4^+

29. proton donors: H_2O and NH_4^+
proton acceptors: OH^- and NH_3

30. $HCl(aq) + NaOH(aq) \rightarrow NaCl(aq) + H_2O(l)$

31. $H_3O^+(aq) + Cl^-(aq) + Na^+(aq) +$
     $OH^-(aq) \rightarrow Na^+(aq) + Cl^-(aq) + 2H_2O(l)$

32. $H_3O^+(aq) + OH^-(aq) \rightarrow 2H_2O(l)$

33. HIO_3, HIO, HIO_4

34. HIO, HIO_3, HIO_4

35. A strong acid ionizes completely in an aqueous solution. A weak acid does not ionize completely in aqueous solution. Its aqueous solution contains hydronium ions, anions, and dissolved acid molecules.

36. Sulfur trioxide, SO_3, is produced as a gas and dissolves in the water vapor in clouds to produce a sulfuric acid solution that falls to the ground as rain or snow. $SO_3(g) + H_2O(l) \rightarrow H_2SO_4(aq)$

37. Have a sour taste; change the color of acid-base indicators; some react with active metals to release hydrogen gas; react with bases to produce salts and water; conduct electric current

38. $H_3PO_4(aq) + H_2O(l) \rightleftarrows$
          $H_3O^+(aq) + H_2PO_4^- (aq)$
$H_2PO_4^-(aq) + H_2O(l) \rightleftarrows H_3O^+(aq) + HPO_4^{2-}(aq)$
$HPO_4^{2-}(aq) + H_2O(l) \rightleftarrows H_3O^+(aq) + PO_4^{3-}(aq)$

16 *Acid-Base Titration and pH,* pp. 61–64

1. d   **5.** a
2. b   **6.** b
3. d   **7.** a
4. c   **8.** d
9. self-ionization
10. basic
11. transition interval
12. pH
13. 10^{-14}
14. 14
15. decreases
16. end point
17. higher
18. lower
19. primary standard
20. higher
21. acidic

22. acidic

23. acidic

24. basic

25. basic

26. A pH meter measures the pH of a solution by measuring the voltage between the two electrodes that are placed in the solution. This works because the voltage is proportional to the hydronium ion concentration.

27. The pH changes slowly at first, then rapidly through the equivalence point, then slowly again.

28. $HIn + H_2O \rightleftarrows H_3O^+ + In^-$
In acidic solution, the H_3O^+ ions in solution drive this equation to the left. HIn is a different color from In^-. HIn is present in acidic solution. In^- is present in basic solution.

29. acidic

30. neutral

31. basic

32. basic

33. basic

34. $[H_3O^+] = 1 \times 10^{-4}$ M;
$[OH^-] = 1 \times 10^{-10}$ M

35. $[H_3O^+] = 1.0 \times 10^{-10}$ M;
$[OH^-] = 1.0 \times 10^{-4}$ M

36. $[H_3O^+] = 5.0 \times 10^{-11}$ M;
$[OH^-] = 2.0 \times 10^{-4}$ M

37. $[H_3O^+] = 1 \times 10^{-4}$ M;
$[OH^-] = 1 \times 10^{-10}$ M

38. $[H_3O^+] = 5 \times 10^{-3}$ M;
$[OH^-] = 2 \times 10^{-12}$ M

39. 1×10^{-5} M

40. 4.0

41. 2.5×10^{-2} M

42. 0.232 M

43. 2.01 M

44. 0.0175 M

17 *Reaction Energy and Reaction Kinetics,* pp. 65–68

1. a   **5.** b
2. d   **6.** a
3. d   **7.** a
4. b   **8.** c
9. reaction mechanism
10. thermochemistry
11. temperature
12. enthalpy
13. temperature
14. joules
15. heat
16. molar heat of formation

17. catalyst
18. $R = k[A][B]^2$, quadrupled
19. f
20. d
21. b
22. e
23. c
24. Homogeneous reactions involve reactants and products that exist in a single phase. Heterogeneous reactions involve reactants in two different phases.
25. The energy of the activated complex is greater than the energy of the reactants and greater than the energy of the products.
26. Nature of reactants; surface area; temperature; concentration; presence of catalysts
27. Entropy is a measure of the degree of randomness of the particles in a system. In nature, processes tend to proceed in the direction that increases the disorder of a system. Therefore, a reaction in which entropy increases is more likely to occur than one in which entropy decreases.
28. In an endothermic reaction, energy is absorbed as heat, and the enthalpy of the reactants is lower than the enthalpy of the products. Therefore, the enthalpy change is positive. In an exothermic reaction, energy is released as heat, and the enthalpy of the products is less than the enthalpy of the reactants. Therefore, the enthalpy change is negative.
29. 215 kJ/mol
30. −172 kJ/mol
31. 0.069 J/g · K
32. −150 kJ/mol
33. −104.5 kJ/mol
34. above 333 K

18 Chemical Equilibrium, *pp. 69–72*

1. a
2. b
3. d
4. b
5. b
6. b
7. a
8. basic
9. $2H_2O(l) \rightleftarrows H_3O^+(aq) + OH^-(aq)$
10. dissolved ions
11. dynamic
12. $K = [Pb^+][NO_3^-]$
13. common-ion effect
14. remains nearly constant
15. equal to
16. denominator

17. $K = \dfrac{[NH_4^+][OH^-]}{[NH_3]}$
18. reverse
19. gas phase
20. anion hydrolysis
21. buffered
22. $K_a = \dfrac{[H_3O^+][A^-]}{[HA]}$
23. changes in concentration, changes in pressure, changes in temperature
24. If a product is precipitated as a solid; if a gaseous product forms and escapes; if a soluble product is only slightly ionized
25. none
26. equilibrium shifts toward the left (reverse reaction is favored)
27. equilibrium shifts toward the right (forward reaction is favored)
28. neutral
29. acidic
30. basic
31. neutral
32. acidic
33. effective buffer
34. ineffective buffer
35. ineffective buffer
36. effective buffer
37. 0.20
38. 3.5
39. 1.79×10^{-3} mol/L
40. 1.2×10^{-8}
41. 8.5×10^{-17} mol/L
42. 6.0×10^{-11}; no

19 Oxidation-Reduction Reactions, *pp. 73–76*

1. b
2. a
3. d
4. b
5. a
6. d
7. b
8. b
9. cathode
10. reduced
11. −1
12. electrochemistry
13. electrical energy
14. +4
15. water and oxygen
16. anode
17. autooxidation
18. voltaic cell
19. anode
20. electrode potential
21. electroplating

22. standard hydrogen electrode
23. decrease
24. reduction
25. reduction
26. oxidation
27. $Ca = +2; C = +4; O = -2$
28. $Fe = +2; N = +5; O = -2$
29. redox
30. nonredox
31. redox
32. 2.23 V, will occur
33. 1.27 V, will occur
34. −2.28 V, will not occur
35. 1.02 V, will occur
36. zinc
37. $Cu^{2+} + 2e^- \rightarrow Cu$
38. copper, zinc
39. zinc, copper
40. $K_2Cr_2O_7 + 14HCl \rightarrow$
$$2KCl + 2CrCl_3 + 7H_2O + 3Cl_2$$

20 *Carbon and Hydrocarbons,*
pp. 77–80

1. d   5. b
2. b   6. b
3. c   7. d
4. d   8. a
9. diamond
10. delocalized electrons
11. catenation
12. saturated
13. four
14. increases
15. octane rating
16. heptane
17. heat
18. isomers
19. hydrocarbons
20. *sp*
21. C_nH_{2n}
22. water, energy, carbon dioxide
23. trans
24. Graphite fibers are stronger and stiffer than steel but are less dense. The strength of the bonds within a layer makes graphite difficult to pull apart in the direction parallel to the layers.
25. Fullerenes consist of nearly spherical cages of carbon atoms. The structure resembles that of a soccer ball.
26. Both a structural formula and a molecular formula indicate the number and types of atoms present in a molecule, but a structural formula also shows the bonding arrangement of the atoms.

27. Groups attached to singly bonded carbon atoms are not held to one side of the molecule because single bonds allow free rotation within a molecule.
28. As the number of carbon atoms in alkanes increases, so do their boiling points. In a distillation tower, the products with lower boiling points condense at the top, where it is cooler. The larger fractions with higher boiling points condense and are removed near the bottom of the tower.
29. $CH_3—CH_2—CH_3$
30.

31.

32. $HC{\equiv}C—CH_2—CH_2—CH_3$
33. 1,5-cyclooctadiene
34. 2-butyne
35. 2,4-hexadiene
36. 1-ethyl,4-methylbenzene
37. 3-ethyl,3-methylheptane
38. 2, 2, 3, 3-tetramethylbutane
39. structural isomers
40. geometric isomers

21 *Other Organic Compounds,*
pp. 81–84

1. b   4. c
2. c   5. a
3. b   6. b
7. vulcanization
8. functional group
9. addition
10. substitution
11. e
12. g
13. c
14. a
15. h
16. b
17. f
18. 2-chloro-2-methylpentane
19. ethyl methyl ether
20. methyl ethanoate
21. 1-bromo-1-fluoroethane
22. diethyl ether
23. 2-pentanone
24.

25.

$$
\underset{\displaystyle \overset{|}{Br}}{\overset{\displaystyle \overset{Br}{\overset{|}{}} \quad \overset{Br}{\overset{|}{}}}{Br - C - CH - CH_2 - CH_3}}
$$

26. $CH_3 - CH_2 - CH_2 - CH_2 - O - CH_3$

27.

$$
\overset{\displaystyle \overset{O}{\|}}{CH_3 - CH_2 - CH}
$$

28.

$$
\overset{\displaystyle \overset{O}{\|}}{H - C - OH}
$$

29. $CH_3 - CH_2 - CH_2 - \underset{\displaystyle \underset{CH_2 - CH_2 - CH_3}{|}}{N} - CH_2 - CH_2 - CH_3$

30. condensation
31. substitution
32. addition
33. Hydrogen bonding causes the intermolecular forces to be stronger in alcohols than in alkanes. The molecules do not separate as readily as do alkanes, so more heat energy is required to cause them to boil.
34. Sunlight breaks down CFC-12 and releases free chlorine atoms. The released chlorine reacts with ozone to form ClO and O_2. The ClO combines with atomic oxygen to produce more chlorine atoms. These then react with more ozone molecules. Ozone molecules are consumed in these reactions.
35. In aldehydes, the carbonyl group is attached to a carbon atom at the end of a carbon-atom chain. In ketones, the carbonyl group is attached to carbon atoms within the chain.
36. No, because addition reactions can occur only with unsaturated molecules. Propane is a saturated hydrocarbon.

22 *Nuclear Chemistry,* pp. 85–88

1. d
2. c
3. b
4. a
8. half-life
9. fusion

5. b
6. d
7. c

10. transmutation
11. radioactive decay
12. transuranium elements
13. gamma rays
14. roentgen
15. rems
16. c
17. d
18. b
19. a
20. beta decay
21. electron capture
22. alpha decay
23. positron emission
24. ^4_2He
25. $^{-1}_0e$
26. $^0_{-1}\beta$
27. ^2_1H
28. Artificial radioactive isotopes are isotopes not found naturally on Earth. They are made by artificial transmutation, which involves bombarding stable nuclei with charged and uncharged particles.
29. A sheet of paper can block alpha particles because they are so heavy. Lead or glass must be used to shield against beta particles. Gamma rays can penetrate most materials; lead and concrete must be used to block them.
30. In fission, a very heavy nucleus splits into more stable nuclei of lower mass. A nuclear reactor is a device that uses controlled-fission chain reactions to produce energy or radioactive nuclides.
31. In fusion, nuclei of low mass combine to form a heavier, more-stable nucleus. This uncontrolled reaction, started by heat and pressure produced by a fission reaction, releases enormous quantities of energy when an H-bomb explodes.
32. In a chain reaction, the element that starts the reaction is reproduced later and can start the process again.
33. Shielding, control rods, moderator, fuel, coolant
34. 4.3542×10^{-11} J
35. 0.137 001 amu
36. 1.3670×10^{-12} J/nucleon
37. 0.98 g
38. 19.12 days